*"Transform pain into poems,
Trauma into relief."*

BLEED
AN ANTHOLOGY

iiPUBLISHING

BLEED an anthology
© 2020 Copyright of individual pieces remains with the contributors.

First published 2020

Copyright notice
All rights reserved. No part of this book may be reproduced in any form or by any electronic or mechanical means, including information storage and retrieval systems, without permission in writing from the authors or publisher.

Published by ii Publishing in conjunction with Poetix University

Cover design: tonii
Design and layout: Nupur Nair

Edited by Ahja Fox and Dara Kalima

ISBN: 978-0-578-72228-3

Printed in the United States of America

iiPUBLISHING
New York, NY
www.toniiinc.com

"Bleeding leads to healing."

CONTENTS

CHILDHOOD	1
LOSS	36
RELATIONSHIPS	74
REFLECTION	118
HEALING	164
AUTHORS	210
INDEX	218

A message from Our President

This anthology is no ordinary collection of poems.

These pages contain the words of poets from all around the world who attended a Poetix University workshop called BLEED. In this 7-day workshop students were prompted to confront their deepest fears, pain, and trauma in several unique writing assignments. The students dissected their internal trauma, from the people who hurt them to the experiences that shaped years of pain. In this confrontation of self, they were able to navigate their thoughts and feelings to 'bleed' out their traumas in their poetry and, most importantly, begin to heal from those experiences.

When designing this workshop I realized, physically and spiritually, bleeding is the initial phase of healing. The body expresses both pain and healing with the secretion of blood. The act of bleeding is usually associated with the negative connotation of pain, but it is equally important to acknowledge bleeding as our body's method of repairing and recovering from trauma. Our spiritual existence is no different. When faced with trauma, we have a need to express it. And this expression is how we bleed spiritually.

But I must admit, those moments when we should be 'bleeding' or expressing our feelings, most decide to conceal them, which only masks our wounds temporarily. Eventually, our hidden traumas find their way into our relationships, self-image, and mental health state. And due to it's insiduous nature, this unexpressed pain breeds until it eventually overwhelms our lives.

This was the purpose of this workshop: to bleed through poetic expression. In this process, we turned pain into poems and transformed our traumas into relief.

Allow these words to speak through your own traumatic experiences, so you can vicariously bleed with the poets. It is our hope that you will be able to heal yourself through the poems they have bled.

tonii
President of Poetix University

CHILDHOOD

"Pain is our first teacher."

"...the first time I cried, I think I was five."

It's funny how classrooms are not classified as
> funerals,
Because the first time I cried, I think I was five.
Five fingers intertwined into my mother's own,
As we travelled the path to my new five-hour home.
I was used to being near my mother, but now, for five
> days out of the week, I was being taken to meet
> my Maker.
My Shaker.
My Heart breaker.
My breath stolen like I was tethered to a damn
> ventilator.

Searching for five minutes of peace,
Amid all of the eyes that were staring at me,
Draining monsoons of saline poured from my eyes,
As my new teacher sat me on her lap in an effort to
    soothe me.
But she was not my mother.
Nor did she resemble my mother.
And between the alphabet, story time, and nursery
    rhymes,
In my mind, Kindergarten was a crime.
It stripped me of Home,
And raped me into submission against my will and
    control.
Today, I gasp in mere horror and pain at how a
    classroom could be perceived as a special type
    of trauma.

"Classroom"
Taneeka L. Wilder

"...glasses that held tears trapped between cheeks and frames."

I had to be maybe 10...
See, it was at 9 that we three went to get glasses...
They were my first pair; big, beige and plastic,
they scarred my cheeks because
the bridge of my nose couldn't sustain their size.
Tears always pooled between cheeks and frames...
I still had these glasses when this happened.
So, it was most definitely after the age of 9,
because Mom got her new pair and
Dad got his first pair of readers.
We both lost our glasses virginity.
He couldn't read the writing and I
couldn't see into the distance so,
little did we know about
what was to come of our future.
It was probably 10 because
mom and I fled at 13 and well,
despite the words begging
for the death of their marriage
in my 7-year-old scribble
scrawled in my diary,
the bench marker was the glasses...
the glasses that held tears
trapped between cheeks and frames.
So, it was somewhere likely between 9 and 10,
in fact, it was likely 10 because my big brother and
big sister were both off in college and I,
I was left alone at home with him.
With the monster they didn't have to see...
I mean they knew him longer than me but
they weren't present for his descent
into the bottom of bottles that went as deeply
as the ocean's floor.

They only had hints
of the depths of the anger
that resided at the bottom.
They were too far away to experience this version of him.
So yes, I was likely 10 or even 11, but
I remember being small,
of feeling small,
as he cornered me between the bed and
the end table with the note and the corded phone
while in a drunken fit.
His 40 something frame hovering over my 10-year-old self.
He yelled and screamed at me, about my penmanship.
This was all about my penmanship as I
jotted a message down for him.
*Didn't I know that older drunken eyes could not see
and understand my 10-year-old script?*
How dare I write in such a way?
And all I could say in my 10-year-old voice was,
I'm sorry,
I didn't know
and 10 tears streamed down my face,
tears pooling between cheeks and frames.
While his thunderous voice promised to strike down upon me
something worth crying about as his hand was raised
poised to strike my 10-year-old face.
I braced for contact but thanks to Mom,
the blow never landed
however, the lesson did,
the fear did,
the understanding solidified,
that was the night that my fun father died and
the drunken monster permanently moved in to reside.

"Clear Vision: Always a Monster"
Dara Kalima

"All the shy, quiet ones, whisper fight when you must..."

She told me she used to fight a lot
because she got picked on.
School suspended me so much
I had to do the second grade twice,
she said.

Wish I could wrap my arms
around her little girl self,
my little girl self.
All the shy, quiet ones,
whisper
fight when you must
but
remember,
sometimes people
throw rocks
at still water
just to watch it ripple.

"Reach"
Carla M. Cherry

"He stole what I had yet to know

And I was just six years old…"

He touched me at six years old
He stole what had yet to be formed
He stole what I had yet to know
And I was just six years old
It took me six days for me to tell my mom
Then six years before I understood what he had done
At the time I was just a six-year-old kid who would
      have never expected him to do what he did
The details I'll keep to myself because they are
      sordid

And they turn certain memories of my childhood
    morbid
So I've blocked that time out of my mental orbit
It's the only way I can keep this smile lock and
    loaded
For if I was to think of the time that I was six years
    old
When love was still blind and before my heart turned
    cold
I'll be on my side at the bottom of the A line
Committing suicide re-killing the six-year-old child
    that I keep forgetting already died

"Six"
Meka J. Woods

"I didn't know who you were anymore
I didn't know who I was anymore."

You Fucked Me Up

I mean,
No complaints on no restraints
In teaching me to use my brain
Creative and critical thinking
And repetitive failure is insane but
There were some things so ingrained that I did not
    have to question them

God is God and He makes no mistakes
Sex before marriage is sin
Marriage means forever
And there's no man greater to aspire to be than my
    Dad

Well Dad
And Mom
I spot 3 lies...

As I remove my high school class ring the night you
    said you were removing yourself from our home
Wondering why would I continue cuffing my finger
    by a single link with your name on it
With my name on it
Removing reveries of a man I once aspired to be
When he no longer aspired to be that man I once
    aspired to be

I didn't know who you were anymore
I didn't know who I was anymore
Was it your name I removed from my brain
    or my own?

Flashback sequences to taunts between siblings
I say
"You were adopted after being rejected and left at a
    bus stop"
She says
"You were born out of wedlock"
And at 14, for the first time
I did the math between a spring baby after a fall
    wedding

But I continued to fall for fallacies you two presented
 to my face as facts

So I guess that's two lies
Sex before marriage as sin can be forgiven when
At least you got married and marriage means forever,
 right?

Things fall apart

Flashforward to my own marital problems
Searching for assistance to solve them and only
 finding failures
Finding no example of success
Finding that you were nobody for me to aspire to

I did not choose to be alive
But every day I have to choose to stay alive
Every day digging sand from the sides of the hole you
 dropped me in
Just enough to keep my head above it as it keeps
 pouring in
Pieces of my own broken marriage
Broken home
Broken life from within

Surviving just enough to say
"I'm better than him"
What's better when the bar is so low it's buried
    beneath the skin?

Creative and critical thinking becomes cynicism
When everything I thought was true must be
    deconstructed

Well Dad
And Mom,
I spot 3 lies
And I apologize for my lack of empathy
I'm sure you were the best you could be
But if I now have to search for myself to see
The truth of these 3
Now I question everything

You taught me
God is God and He makes no mistakes

Well,
What if that's a lie like all else you taught me
And God made a mistake
When God made me.

"3 Lies"
Anubis

"I just couldn't believe my eyes..."

For 12 years of my life, my vision was clear.
I had aspirations, creative imaginations,
But leading into the 12th year of my life, those were replaced with fear...

I just couldn't believe my eyes,
No...I just couldn't believe these lies.
Lies was what I saw,
These lies became a flaw,
And it took 12 years before my vision drew it's last straw...

For a long time, I looked up to reaching 12 years of age.
I was gonna sit in the passenger seat and was only a year away from the adolescent teenager.
But when I hit the age of 12, I was hit with a scary reality,
Drowning my sanity,
Changing my mentality,
And degrading my vision, rapidly...

My vision dwindled,
Whenever I squinted,
To make things transparent.

And with every passing day,
And after tears were wiped away,
It was time I faced my fears,
And do what I never wanted to do, for years...

So I went and got some glasses...
But 12 weeks into wearing them
Never cleared my vision
Of a future that wasn't grim.
Because my 12-year-old imagination was just craziness...
I use to think, that a reaper of sight,
Would creep into my room at 12 midnight
To strip my vision of happiness and replace it with fright.
I just always struggled to believe that I obtained a vision of blurriness...

12 years old was a funny age for me when I look back on it.
It took me 12+ years to get over my fear of wearing contacts
But my drive for my original appearance just wouldn't let me submit.
Maybe in time I'll try Lasik or some other form of correction
As I just want to dive into a pool, 12+ feet deep
With a clear mind, clear heart, and a clear vision...

"Fears of Blur"
Kevin P.

"...the pureness was ripped right out of her"

Pain is a feeling that is hard to understand
It is also unusually difficult to comprehend
This is just a general concept of that term
My aforementioned statement is an opinion
There's just one question I have thought on
And even now it bothers me to my very core
"What if you witnessed great pain as a child
And was never able to recover fully from it?"

(on a whole pain can take quite a big toll)

Her pain started relatively early on as a kid
So the intro to pain for her began at age six
She witnessed her father abuse her mother
As a young girl this did leave her feeling lost
This started to make her despise her father
How can somebody whose duty was supposed
To be to honor and protect her and her mom
Dare lay a single finger on the one he "loved"

(to a point you forget that you have a soul)

Pain is difficult the younger you happen to be
It inevitably changes your view on everything
You can lose faith and hope for a normal life
It forces the kind soul to set up a big barrier
Pain can dig in deep and mess someone up
So people will put up barriers and defenses
In order to "cope" with certain life situations
Cause getting your mind off that can be hard

(if pain repeats you won't ever be the same)

Pain dug back into her at the age of fifteen
She was with some friends who she trusted
These few were supposed to have her back
They left her alone in a strange man's home
He took full advantage of her soul and naivety
And the pureness was ripped right out of her
This incident broke her apart just like a mirror
In turn it gave her a fractured view of all men

(as it reminds you that life isn't a fun game)

Pain brings visible scars and invisible wounds
Pain forces you away from what brings you joy
Pain can literally transform your whole mindset
Pain zaps your energy just like a hungry leech
Trauma makes you terrified to share your story
Trauma will force one into their own sanctuary
Trauma makes you forget the person you are
Trauma inevitably can fracture an entire soul
These two things will definitely mess you up
Only if you let them do whatever they please
At times the most terrifying things to a person
Are of course the few details they keep within
But to truly open up about things is really hard
You may never know what all people deal with
If those dark things aren't brought to the light
Scars will serve as a reminder of the damage
But the wounds that hurt most you won't see...

"On High Alert"
Mike Cruz

"...how to live in the world filled with monsters."

sometimes i look at you and i don't see love.
i see the hate you carried around for my father.
maybe pain.
probably because you see his face in me—well in all
    of us.
but i always got a different love from you.
why am i not this?
why am i not that?
well, maybe because i have been broken for nearly my
    entire life
and i never got to see you as a happy wife
and i can't seem to satisfy you as your daughter
even though you should be proud because you taught
    her...
how to live in this world filled with monsters.
so i thought...
you and i fought and fought
and you still never really heard my cry
my youth passed me by
you didn't even know that i was in pain.
your only little girl.

you were supposed to protect me from this world
not make me feel guilty for the things i didn't learn
or should i say the things you didn't teach...
and i get it, you had a fucked up childhood filled with
    loss and trauma
i sensed it all around your aura
but that should've given you more fight
you should've saw the light
and the blessings God gave you
instead you gave me the coldest shoulder
that night you got the news...
my sister died and that finished you
and finished me with the same blow
ever since that night
the last little bit of light
was taken.
you blamed yourself for having lost your daughter
because you thought you never fought for her
and it's fucked up because i needed you still
i was 11.
getting bullied at a new school
with new rules
and a bunch of kids who were fools
who thought it was cool
to judge me.

you didn't even notice.
i cut school at the age of 12
as a cry for help
because you didn't see me.
if it wasn't for you looking over your back constantly
and shutting down honestly
we would've been at a better moment presently.
by the age of 15
i felt what a man was supposed to feel like
and i smoked weed
that's when it hit me
i knew life was a bitch
i was blowing trees
just so i can go through the days
in a daze and worry free.
i was more outside and less at home
because of the mom i had woulda much rather be
    alone.
16 and 17 were kind of a blur
but that's what i prefer
since they were so dark i chose to keep it in me
until i turned 18 and learned that not everyone is
    against me
by the time i was 19
i thought i was in love and became pregnant

a blessing.
your grandchild,
and i still didn't quite know how to make it worth
    your while...
i decided to tell you,
but i moved out because i wanted a home
where love was the only language we spoke
but instead you cried to me
and chose to help me instead.
you swept all my pain under your rug of more pain
so now there's this pile of dirt
just waiting to come out
and i find myself 25 now
still trying to find the perfect words to say
so you can attempt to understand the growing pains
and self-taught lessons that i went through
but still i find myself feeling like i'm better off alone
    in this pursuit.

"Page 32"
Aly Marie

"I need saving, we need healing"

Fire intrigued me,
Fistfights at school set me back,
Anger consumed me
It wasn't my fault,
Troubled child misunderstood,
I needed saving
We needed healing,
Baby raising a baby,

Mom did what she could
Escaping abuse,
Wherever she goes, I go
Just my mom and me
Her strength carried us,
I learned to be strong from her,
My stubbornness too
We were both troubled,
Making it through the darkness,
Surviving it all.

"Troubled Child"
Latonica Readdy

"For ten hours I tossed and turned like a leaf in the wind"

Even more than ten vanilla smothered fingertips
from the cinnamon buns Daddy bought my sister
    and I
from *Better Crust Pie* on Saturday afternoons
after our piano lessons at Harlem School of the Arts,
we loved Black Liberation Bookstore on Lenox and
    131st.
Meandered the aisles longer than the ten minutes
    Daddy gave us to find something to buy.
He'd have us read excerpts of the books we wanted
    to Ms. Mulzac.
Daddy's smile was ten times brighter than Sirius A
    at our polysyllabic prowess.

I was ten when my eyes landed on a white cover---
an unsmiling brown girl with downcast eyes
wearing ribbons the color of marigolds
holding a white doll by the neck.
The Bluest Eye.
I put it on the top of my stack of ten at the register.
Grinned at the clicks of the calculator.
Tapped all ten fingers in anticipation.
I started reading it that night.
On the third page, it is revealed that Pecola is
    having her father's baby.

I put the book down.
For ten hours I tossed and turned like a leaf in
    the wind
terrified I'd dream about a world
where little black girls didn't have a daddy
whose arms were branches to hang from
whose lap was a safe space to snuggle,
listen to his heart thump against his chest.
Our hands in Daddy's were an unspoken
    I love you.

I wrote Daddy a letter ten lines long explaining
    why I could not read this book.
Slipped it inside and put it on my mother's dresser
    next to her mirrored tray
with ten dancing angels where she kept her
    perfumes.

I found my copy of *The Bluest Eye* when I was
    sixteen.
Must have read it at least ten times.
Ever since then my heart has been breaking
for little black girls
who are violated by men
who are supposed to love and protect them
and fields where marigolds refuse to grow.

"Innocence Lost"
Carla M. Cherry

"She creates her own world of bliss."

During her early and most formative years,
There were those that called her WEIRD.
Teased and mocked was she,
For being DIFFERENT,
For talking proper,
For using her VOICE to think outside the ring of
    normative thought,
From her BODY seen as too thin or too skinny
    to LOVE,
To her hair not being long enough, straight enough,
    and "too kinky."
It would've made one's SELF-WORTH,
Plummet deeper than the waters that houses
    plankton and seaweed.
From the vile words thrown at her, she laughed,
Because deep down, these words had nothing to
    do with her.
From learning the difference between the REAL
    and COUNTERFEIT,

To understand the healing power of self-love,
    self-care, self-harmony, and her God-given
    voice.
She is molded and shouldered by the dust that was
    thrown at her.
For every despair she encounters,
She knows she is strong enough to continue to
    move forward.
Never weighed down by the poisonous mindset
    of others.
She evolves.
She lifts.
She creates her own world of bliss.
She is not deterred,
For the power within her will always burn.
Hope is her medicine.
Peace is her sword.
Healing is her nourishment...the sweetest
    and most beautiful rebellion and She-Volution.

"She-Volution"
Taneeka L. Wilder

"...feelings changing, hearts dissolving."

There was a time when my heart was getting older,
feeling numb around the world a bit colder.
The era of teenage was hitting me hard,
going through the changes of the world like
      a hazard.
The things I felt could never have been expressed,
even I was so shy that I would keep it suppressed.

This led me to an eternal journey
of heartbreaks, emotional distress,
where I would get anxious and depressed.
People changing, days evolving,
feelings changing, hearts dissolving.
Losing personality to become another,
unresolved childhood issues became a cover.
Was drowning in the failures sinkage,
was trying to find out the way of being teenage.

"Era of Teenage"
Dhruvil Purani

"I was 9 years old when I first learned how to hate my body."

I was 9 years old when I first learned how to
    hate my body.
I remember standing in the schoolyard.
The kids wouldn't play with me because I had
    put on a few extra pounds over the summer.
This fifth grader came up to me and just started
    calling me ugly and fat.
I cried nine times after that.
In front of those girls
In the bathroom
On the way home from school
While watching cartoons
During dinner
While taking a shower and that was the
    worst part.
I looked at my body and I hated it more and more.
Before bed.
When waking up the next morning

And during recess when it would start
    all over again.
Mami told me I was pretty but I couldn't shop for
    jeans in the kids stores anymore.
I had a body suddenly and womanly hips were way
    too large for those cute rhinestone jeans I
    saw in the window.
Nine pairs of jeans later, I found a pair that fit.

I never forgot that gutting feeling.
The reasons to hate my body increased with time.
I looked at my growing hips like they were a crime.
How I wished to fold myself away, one piece
    of skin at a time. Nine times over.
It took me nine years to:
Get past the trauma
Slowly start loving myself
Accept that what the bullies said aren't
    a reflection of myself
To not want to be anybody else.

"Untitled 1"
Jessica Collazo

"feeling like all these rocks in this city already made of concrete"

I was four years old when I used to see my mother cry
and feel her sorrows lie
heavy on my shoulders
feeling like all these rocks
in this city already made of concrete...
I tried to act like I didn't notice
because she'd be ashamed
and that's when it ate me.
I was only 4 years old when I heard my father yell at
    my mother.
4 times before he hit her.
I ran.
my brothers covered me
as we were scared
we didn't know what next
but God I know you were there

because you heard me.
at 4 years old my body froze
but my heart was voiced
because I yelled so loud
you heard your child cry
and you came and saved me.
I've lost the light again.
since then
I'm on a hunt to find me.
searching for the pieces that were broken
way before any man can ever come close to me.
but Father please forgive me
I'm going through more growing pains
and learning things again
and I'm sorry i haven't sought you
but since 4 years old you been there
my only knight in shining armor.

"Page 26"
Aly Maria

"I wasted the best years of my life waiting for your repreieve."

You taught me how to leave.
Grieve.
I wasted the best years of my life waiting for your
    reprieve.
But it never came.
Packed bags and silent goodbyes.
I tried to understand why.
Why did you leave without a formal farewell?
I caught myself curling up into a shell
Seething in these feelings of anger, hurt
You disappearing.
No room for healing.

You taught me how to leave.
I had to teach myself how to stay.
Feet planted firm on the ground.
I know what I want now---and I'll do my best to never
     make her cry
To make her question why I walked out without
     saying goodbye
I want my children to know what love can be.

"Untitled 2"
Jessica Collazo

LOSS

"There is gain in every loss."

"Excuse me, my mother was killed; she didn't just die..."

I can't recall the first time I cried;
but what I do know is that
I was only 2 years old when my mom died.
Excuse me, my mother was killed;
she didn't just die...
and that's the shit that would keep me up
all through the night!

Bitter, angry, sad and confused;
an emotional wreck I can admit.
Rejected love in exchange for abuse,
but how could I know the difference?
After all, I was just a kid
and I did what kids did,
I blamed myself, they said don't do it but
I didn't listen because;
I was only 2 years old when my mom died,
but I cannot recall the first time I cried.

"Untitled 3"
LaDasha-Diamond

"I slept beside disdain
Ate breakfast with your volatility"

Maybe the pain started
When she died
And the right to grieve
Was stolen from me
And when restored
It was confined
Or maybe the shock came
When you should've loved me
Unconditionally
But I was never good enough
And I always came home
To a new argument
I slept beside disdain
Ate breakfast with your volatility
Half convinced there would be poison
Half wanting there to be
Maybe the break occurred
When I looked around and realized
That I was placed in the hands
Of people who were supposed to love me

But only sought to bend me to their wills
Or maybe the great distress
Happened every time I jumped
Expecting to be caught
And introduced every shard of me
To the ground
But if I'm being honest
The great trauma began
Before I ever really did
New on this Earth
You were supposed to hold me
But you chose to walk away
Chose to be in peace
Chose not to fight for me
I have wondered if I'm worth it ever since
And maybe sometimes
I look at my hummingbird reflection
Never landing; not allowing
Anyone to know me
And maybe every time someone leaves
I watch them retreat in to your shadow
I can't tell the darkness apart anymore
But I'm trying

"Original Sin"
Luna Brasa

"...9 years old was the first time I truly felt dormant in my own body"

Age 9 was the first known time that I pressed pause on my grieving
At age 9, I froze up on my healing and my mind swarmed with confusion
My grandmother passed away and I didn't know how to process it
At age 9, you'd think that I would be good at expressing my emotions, but 9 years old was the first time I truly felt dormant in my own body
The entire world shook and I was the only one who felt it
What was I supposed to do? How was I supposed to feel? How was I supposed to handle this loss?
The matriarch of my maternal bloodline left me before I could ever ask her for proper advice and guidance on life
At 9 years old, I opted to not go to my grandmother's funeral and I've regretted it ever since

I told my mom that I wasn't feeling well and I didn't
    want to go, she didn't push though I wish
    that she did
Because the truth is, 9 years old was the age that I
    learned just how much I don't like letting go
Saying goodbye is difficult for me and each time feels
    like a funeral
Death weighs heavy on my heart like a ton of bricks
    and I am left broken, crying to be fixed
I don't like being alone and it all started when I was
    9 years old and had to let go of everything
I've ever known
At 9 years old, I chose not to go to my grandmother's
    funeral because burying her made it real
    and I didn't want to feel that pain
In my mind, if I felt the pain then it would be true so
    I didn't go to the burial
But still, to this day, whenever I have to let go of
    someone special to me, I am left crying and
    cradling that 9-year-old little girl inside.

"Age 9: Loss of a Matriarch"
Latonica Readdy

"Stuck in skin that always Fit just a little too tight"

Just a shy kid
Stuck in skin that always
Fit just a little too tight
Stuck in a world I couldn't
Make right
Because it wasn't home
You were my north star, my
Guiding light
The most radiant point in
The night sky
No wonder you led us all into
Your orbit
Our world imploded in your
Absence

We haven't been the same since
Becoming strangers we don't recognize
Desperate fingertips lead to
Drastic measures
And I don't even know
Anymore
We keep orbiting, not sure
What to do with the space you
Left behind
Just a shy kid
Making sense of the world
With a pen
And these words in my soul
Just a shy kid
Going through this on my own
Or as luck would have it
Maybe not as alone
As I thought

"Just a Shy Kid"
Luna Brasa

"Goodbye self loathing
And fuck you with forgiveness"

You hate me
You have been angry with me ever since I could remember
Which I suppose isn't so long since I can only remember as far back as when Grampa died

After repass, I remember searching for him in his church until I remembered
He wasn't there
16 years ago

Is that when you began to hate me?

I don't think so
I montage between tears
"Jesus Walks" in my ears
Until "All Falls Down" on senior trips
'Til I remember he won't be at my Graduation

But that wasn't it

Did you begin to hate me that summer?
Cut scenes between hanging out in a feature film production loft,
Hanging out at home on the couch with pops,
Freshmen orientation accompanied by "Late Registration" while hiding out in a feature film production loft
After pops left our couch for a couch in another home

Did you begin to hate me then?

Or a year later when university secretly put me on suicide watch when grades dropped
Returning a year later just to drop out
Only to drop into orgasms and alcohol

With women with attachment issues
Never knowing who's coming or going

But I thought you loved me then
You smiled a devilish smile/ grin

Or did you hate me when I made a plan for God to
    laugh at?
An order of operations for a rebirth aborted by "love"

Get a degree, get a good job, get an apartment, get
    married, have children
Became
Get married, have children---forget the rest and watch
    someone else get it

Is that when you began to hate me,
Mr. Reflection?

Reflecting on every mistake I made
Making more by bowing to you out of reflex
Forcing me to reflect on ev'ry mistake I would make
    in a daze
Hypnotized by tracked trains
Contemplating release

I'm done contemplating, Mr. Reflection

I release myself from you

Goodbye self hate
Goodbye self loathing
And fuck you with forgiveness
Until we make love
Until I make me love me
Because I'm lovely
Without you

"Mr. Reflection"
Anubis

"You injected that inferior poison into my veins"

I once had a dream.
Once pristine, shiny and hopeful,
Now shattered glass at my feet.
It was one of my lowest points.
I had a future planned out.
Protect and serve
But you told me I wasn't qualified.
A girl fresh out of college wasn't good enough.

Do you know what you're getting into?
That's what you asked me.
You injected that inferior poison into my veins
And I've been trying to flush it out ever since.
I second guess everything.
Fearful of rejection—
Has left me broken and drowning in tension.

"Untitled 4"
Jessica Collazo

"I wasn't always sure but definitely picky with who I let inside of me..."

The most cutthroat experiences are seen not heard and
    hidden in plain sight
The darkest of secrets are never spoken of though
    hidden just below the surface if only you
    knew where to look
For me, I was too afraid to look the night you infected
    me
I wasn't always sure but definitely picky with who I
    let inside of me because I knew of the power I
    held
What lies between my thighs is an unworthy man's
    genocide, so they don't dare step to me
But some men are monsters and demons who find
    their way through the defense mechanisms,
    pass the fortresses, and damage the very core
    of a paradise and renders it of its sunshine
    without warning
You, the sorcery of a man, damaged my paradise
    before I could ever watch it bloom into a
    civilization

You set my space on fire without any consideration or
 reason yet had the nerve to look at me in
 my eyes with a fake empathetic guilty look on
 your face and say that I'm going to regret
 being with you
Never giving me an explanation as to what you meant
You left me to find out two years later just how much
 of a massacre you've made out of my body
As a teenage girl, I thought older men knew better
 until I came across you and realized that real
 men with commonsense don't mess with little
 girls
You didn't have to do what you did to me but of
 course, that didn't matter to you
I guess you decided a long time ago to get back at
 young girls as a way of revenge for what
 happened to you
It didn't matter to you if I wanted a husband and kids
 because to you I was to blame just as
 much as the girl who infected you
There is no excuse for you plaguing my sanity and
 peace of mind

I can still remember the exact day when I lost myself;
    the gynecologist told me that the test
    came back positive
My vision became blurry and a ringing in my ear
    prevented me from hearing any voice of
    reason or consolidation
All I knew was that I needed to get home as fast as I
    could
I nearly got hit by a car twice while trying not to
    break down in the middle of the street
The mental beatings couldn't have come any quicker;
    my room became a dark dungeon in a
    blink of an eye
How could I let this happen? He didn't have to do that
    to me
Who's going to love me once they know that I'm
    burning? I feel like a town whore
Destructive thoughts constantly stalked me like the
    shadows on my walls, if they could talk
    they'd be screaming

I lost myself for years because of what you did to me
My voice, my dignity, and my self-confidence were all gone
I didn't want to be seen by anybody, I felt dirty and disgusting
If it wasn't for Spirit guiding me, I would have been dead a long time ago
I stepped into my 20's with transparency and honesty
I found that I am still worthy of being loved, respected, and wanted
You didn't win
You tried and failed
You may have burned the land back then but it has been restored
You lose
Though I am still healing and nurturing that teenage girl back to love
I have gained the majority of myself back and can say that I've earned my victory

"A Letter to my Infector: You Lose"
Latonica Readdy

"I'm learning to live fully, joyfully, without you, but it's like soul music with no bass"

My imaginary friend wasn't long for this world---
as soon as you were talking and walking
I had somebody to blow bubbles with.
Took turns jumping off the toilet into the tub
and watching suds splash onto the floor.
Because your twin bed was next to mine,
I never was that afraid of the dark.

My dolls had your dolls to talk to.
I had somebody to wait for daybreak with,
to open presents on Christmas,
and for Saturday morning cartoons,
whose voice blended with mine for Josie and the
      Pussycats.
Watched movies on HBO until we could recite the
      lines from memory in unison.
Roller skated through the house.
Fought, but shared everything from books to stories
      about boy-crushes.

When Daddy's cancer declared war on his marrow,
we took turns crying. Cooking. Doing his laundry.
Telling ourselves he wouldn't die.
When he stopped eating, we bathed his skin.
Brushed his hair. Clipped his nails.
Smiled at him the last time he opened his eyes.
It felt like the end of the world.

We wondered how we could go on but trees bend in
      the wind,
their roots firm in the ground.
We learned to laugh about our pillow fights with
      Daddy and
our backseat beatings when our mouths got too fresh.

We raised our children like they were siblings,
      passing on the wisdom passed down to us.
We'd grow old together like Sadie and Bessie Delany.
We're still together, we croaked, and cracked up.

Nothing has been the same since the day your doctor
      said
he'd never seen a tumor like yours in the eighteen
      years he'd been in practice.
No matter how much I prayed through your eleven
      hour surgery
to remove a quarter of the muscle in your thigh,
sat by your beside in the ICU, through your near
      kidney failure, dialysis,
physical therapy as you learned how to walk again,
I could not stop the metastasis into your lungs, brain,
      and eyes.
No matter how hard you fought to stay with Mommy,
      me, your daughter, my son,
God took you home at age of 44.
I know your soul is at peace.
Mine's is not.
I saw you almost every day
during the six months you were in the hospital
and I still kick myself for not spending the night the
      two times you asked
because I just wanted to sleep so I could get through
      the day at work.
I miss your jokes.
Our hours long talks on the phone
even though my house was five minutes from yours.

I'm learning to live fully, joyfully, without you, but
      it's like soul music with no bass.
Smelling a rose with no scent.
The sky without moon or stars.
A field without grass.
The ocean without waves.
A diamond without light.

"Dear Donna"
Carla M. Cherry

"I just lay still. Waiting for it to consume me"

It's been a year now,
Since I was diagnosed with this deadly Grief.

Although it arrived like a storm,
It hit me one bone at a time,
Navigating its way through my veins,
Dissolving its poison in my blood.

I detected the denial at first,
Fooling me into believing,
That this was my imagination,
Playing tricks on me,
Eventually planning to leave.

But Grief stayed,
Decomposing into anger,
A rage so red and intense,
My spine started to quiver,
Begging for solitude if not mercy.

You see that was my bargaining talking.
'Give me solitude if not mercy,
Grant me distraction if not a breath,
Take me instead...'

Evidently this didn't work,
Opening the doors to my depression,
This stage didn't make me beg anymore,
In fact it made me do nothing.
I just lay still. Waiting for it to consume me.

It feels like decades now,
Since I have been stuck in this void.
However,

I think I see someone else coming in,

I think she calls herself 'Acceptance'.

This Acceptance.

She wore Grief in volumes,
Draping them on herself,
Like her priced ornaments.

I asked her to teach me how.

First,
She lifted my bleeding heart,
And plastered it with sweet memories.
Yours.

Next,
She collected my tears like tonic,
Replacing their salty regret,
With honey flavoured remembrance.
Yours.

Finally,
She redecorated my loss,
Embroidering on it,
Your laugh, your songs,
And your heart on mine,
Where it belongs.

And then I wore my Grief,
Never again asking it to leave.

"Finding the Cure"
Nupur Nair

"Go ahead and kill me."

I'm thinking in my mind oh my is it my time to die? I didn't even fully get to live my life, now you coming with the threat of homicide, only question that I have to ask is why? So much I planned to do, so many people to meet but now you at me with that ratchet about to have me 6 ft. deep. What will my family think, what will all my friends say?

Full of hurt, shock and mourning, begging for another day just to say, I love you. Yet, I'm headed for an early tomb, fuck it! Go ahead and kill me, I got nothing to lose, send my body back to the dirt but God gets my soul. Look me in my eyes, can't you see that I'm cold? Chills got me shivering because I'm naked in winter. Don't matter if I lose the battle 'cause at the war, I was a winner. I can die knowing I was solid and stayed away from pretenders. Lord, please forgive them, I ain't judging because we're all sinners.

"Untitled 5"
LaDasha-Diamond

"Hear me now
As I take my gifts to Heaven"

Words spoken before my last breath
A simple woman
A simple goodbye
A poetic woman recites
Remember happiness is essential
Sunrise smiles at me
Moon hugs my fears
Mother nature collecting my tears
Hear me now
As I take my gifts to Heaven

Continuing my purpose
Helping, supporting, and loving
Crow's wicked eyes
Awaiting innocent flesh
My soul protected
Devil's invitation of descending below
Let me convey to you all
How happiness and kindness is the way
It's who you have
It's living with no regrets

It's the wisdom gained
It's realizing
Bad is temporary
It's making beautiful memories
Lasting for eternity
It's taking risks
Risks that bloom into success
When some risks don't bloom
The opportunity
Will present itself later

It's trusting his divine plan for your life
Happiness is unconditional love
What I have for you all
Doing what you love and with those you love
It's being vulnerable about your feelings
It's being open and honest
It's about taking chances
Happiness is giving all of me to all of you
Happiness is about speaking your mind
Not caring about what anyone thinks

Happiness is being able to say a special, "thank you"
"I appreciate you"
What I always said,
"How lovely!"
When I was deeply touched
Happiness is confidence
In what you want to achieve
Happiness is finding out who I am
My purpose in this world
Witnessing living my purpose

The appreciation reciprocated
The love given and shared
The forgiveness expressed
The genuine friendships and relationships
Happiness is having the best parents
The best siblings
The best kids and husband
People who don't give up on those they love
My journey has been painful
Beautiful and rewarding

Filled with hugs, kisses, and heartfelt words
Happiness is feeling at peace with myself
As I breathe my last breaths
Let me embrace all the sweetness
Let me reminisce
Let me let go of pain
Rejoicing about my new journey
Let me express how happy I am
Leaving my words, creativity, and legacy
Filled with gratitude

Grateful for the struggles and trials
Let me reassure you all
I'm not sad
I'll live on through the memories
Through the pictures and my books
Through my beliefs and sayings
My name Coco
Will echo for an eternity
All the good sprinkled
All the kindness shared

Through all the pain
To my three children
Promise me three things
One to pray everyday
It's the strongest medicine
Best communication

Answer to everything
Two is to remember how much I love you
Remember how passionately I loved
Three is to remember a collage of me

My heartbeat and voice
My laughter and happiness
My cries and determination
My cooking and sayings
My hugs and kisses
My beliefs and values
My smile and advice
My support and resilience
My faith and hope
My forgiveness and weaknesses

My imperfections
My trials and truth
My will to live
For the three of you
Most difficult for me
You see
Releasing all this
To set my soul free
Knowing I did my best
To nurture our family tree.

"Don't Cry For Me"
Keisha Molby-Baez

> "I would rather be swallowed in wholes, than a half-space punctuated with breaks."

In piercing isolation, I cradled my corpse with praise and adulation.
Others thought I was mad or had gone insane,
But the imprisonment of their cognitions,
Emitting from their neurological structures,
Failed to perceive Beauty in ruins and rupture.
The damage that has been transmitted from generation to generation,
The hatred that's been taught to stunt a starving nation,
Is the demolition that is needed in order to unite with our higher selves and Creation.

So I can cradle my corpse,
And kiss it with my lips,
Knowing I will die many, many deaths once more
    again.
And until that day comes,
I can look at where I've been,
To rise beyond my pain,
To take fear by the reins,
And be proud of the woman I have gained.
With tears down my face,
And a smile gently placed,
I would rather be swallowed in wholes, than a
    half-space punctuated with breaks.
For I am the culmination of both Sun, Shadow, and
    Space.

"Sun, Shadow, & Space"
Taneeka L. Wilder

"...that's 7 kisses that will never touch my face. 7 hugs that won't ever be embraced."

After 7 years on this earth, I had to deal
With grappling the fact,
That you weren't coming back;
It didn't seem real.

But I had no choice in the matter,
'Cause after 7 plus years, some of my heart is still
     shattered.

Broken in 7 pieces that I can't ever pick up.
'Cause even in my adult years,
The road has still been tough.

'Cause that's 7 kisses that will never touch my face.
7 hugs that won't ever be embraced.
7 memories that won't ever be erased.
7 "I love you's" that would never be replaced.

"I Miss You"
Cheree Alexander-Velez

**"Allow regret to disappear as the dew,
take in rest as the light of the moon..."**

I will not say do not mourn me
when my body fails.
If there is no grief,
it will mean
you never needed me after all.
Do not mourn for long
as it will not change a thing—
this body will not come back
and you will only have squandered that time.
I would tell you I will miss you, but
that won't be true
because I will still be right next to you.

I will be the breeze rustling your hair,
the rain drops that kiss your cheek,
the warm rays of the sun that comfort you,
the voice of the birds that sing.
I will still be with you to teach
some of life's learnings—
Allow regret to disappear as the dew,
take in rest as the light of the moon,
love without end as the ocean's horizon,
listen and observe as the doe in the meadow.
Release my ashes to nurture the Earth
and hold out your arms love
to welcome me home.

"Untitled 6"
Lea Elani

"You had to leave me before I turned ONE."

PART 1A: SELF REFLECTION
My life has been an eventful ride
Now I have to take things in stride
Due to my age we never even met
I live a life with endless fear & regret
If I had an option to escape the night
I just know that you would be my light
You had to leave me before I turned ONE
If you was here we would have lots of fun
If we're talking creatively I am just like you
And that's one fact that I know to be true

PART 1B: MY FATHER
Of course I have to start with my other half
My dad told me that you were truly creative
He would bring up that you were really social
He knew a woman of style when he saw you
He loved to bring up just how caring you were
There was still ONE thing I didn't know though

And that was how our real bond actually was
He told me that you was an amazing mother
You'd say how blessed you were to have me

And that in itself is something I take pride in
By just hearing that you still really loved me

PART 2A: SELF REFLECTION
My life has been an eventful ride
Now I have to take things in stride
Due to my age we never even met
I live a life with endless fear & regret
If I had an option to escape the night
I just know that you would be my light
You had to leave me before I turned ONE
If you was here we would have lots of fun
If we're talking creatively I am just like you
And that's one fact that I know to be true

PART 2B: MY GRANDPARENTS
The next up are the ones who gave you life
They have told me you were a sweetheart
They told me your smile could light up a room
They mentioned to me you were a good soul
My grandma tells me you are a special ONE
I had to ask them about how she was with me
Both were born in PR so this is what they said

> Deberías saber que tu madre
> realmente te amaba

This is the only thing that I needed to hear
There's one thing I treasure about my mother
It was her wholesome nature & her big heart

PART 3A: SELF REFLECTION
My life has been an eventful ride
Now I have to take things in stride
Due to my age we never even met
I live a life with endless fear & regret
If I had an option to escape the night
I just know that you would be my light
You had to leave me before I turned ONE
If you was here we would have lots of fun
If we're talking creatively I am just like you
And that's one fact that I know to be true

PART 3B: MY AUNTS
It's necessary to tell what I got from my aunts
So here's what I found out by talks with them
They told me you were such a genuine person
They constantly told me you were so beautiful
They would always tell me that you were loving
My aunts also said that she was a special ONE

As tears rolled they said you really adored me
Hearing that from everyone I asked matters

It gives me a newfound sense of my purpose
My heart just wishes that I could have met you
I love you so much & that is a fact that is true

PART 4A: SELF REFLECTION
My life has been an eventful ride
Now I have to take things in stride
Due to my age we never even met
I live a life with endless fear & regret
If I had an option to escape the night
I just know that you would be my light
You had to leave me before I turned ONE
If you was here we would have lots of fun
If we're talking creatively I am just like you
And that's one fact that I know to be true

PART 4B: I LOVE YOU...
If you're up there I got something to tell you
So best believe what I have to say to be true
Despite God taking you from me at age ONE
I have had a great life & was never truly alone
I lost you so young so there is an obvious rift
If you must know I did inherit your creative gift
Not having you physically here makes me sad
In a way I'm still a part of you so I can be glad

It's my turn to carry The Creativity Crown
Since I'm a man who is fully aware & grown

No longer having to ask questions about why
To know that you loved me is enough to get by
You aren't here to show me what I should do
Yet I hope that you do know that... I LOVE YOU

"You Live In Me"
Mike Cruz

RELATIONSHIP

"We give a portion of ourselves to others with a risk of never being whole again."

"I wanted to tell the world that he was a wolf in sheep's clothing"

Three years ago, I was hopeful again.
With few doubts in my eyes,
Whatever became of love's end in the past was buried
    and dead.
Heart once again open,
With childlike wonder,
I was ready to surrender to my heart's slumber.
On paper he seemed great,
And his character appeared astute,
So now was an opportunity to see this through.
I thought he felt the same,
I thought his words were pure,
I told him I hated games, and did not do casual,
    hook-ups, or "flings."

He said he was the same,
But little did I know—it was all a ruse.
Upon his discovery of lies and deceit,
My heart felt the fury of hell.
It left an impact for future stories to tell.
My eyes grew dim,
And for days, I would sit angry, dazed, and confused,
Wondering how I went against my intuition.
I wanted to tell the world that he was a wolf in
      sheep's clothing,
That he pretended to love the black woman,
But privately harbored insecurity, hatred, and shame.
I wondered to myself if I could ever trust another
      with my heart again?
Knowing that love has nothing to do with hurting,
      wounding, or winning.
I just wondered why he couldn't be honest?
Because that is what I gave to him.

"Counterfeit Love"
Taneeka L. Wilder

"...I lay helpless on the ground... slowly starting to fade."

If I were a leaf...would you let me leave?
Would you let me simply break free
From the limbs used to create and nurture me?
The same limbs used to carry,
Caress, and support me
When life wanted nothing more then to drown
Me in tears as the sky came crashing down
All so you could cast shade
As I lay helpless on the ground...slowly starting to
    fade.

Would you leave me be?
Would you let me learn to be me
As I navigate the world's winds, storms,
And dangerous thorns,
In an effort to fly through my own destiny?
Would you let me find love in a journey
As I float in a boundless sea
Searching for what's right for me
Amongst the potential wonder, and beauty?
Or would you rather uproot my visions?
By binding down my every decision...

Would you let me burn?
Would you let this connection between us churn?
Because as it stands
I once wanted your helping hands
But you instead gave resistance
When all I needed was supportive guidance.
You then let the season of Autumn
Affect the outcome
Of what was once a wonderful connection
Split by decisions I've made,
That you wish I didn't.
This would then implant fear
That I may never extract for years
Causing the blood we share
That should be fueling me
To now be the blood we share
That's now draining me...
So if I were a leaf...
I'd hope this falling out between us
Won't carry over between seasons...

"If I Were A Leaf"
Kevin P.

"A stranger to her own identity

For she traded it in years ago to be a part of him."

Hollow girl.
Faking a smile
Telling the world she was fine
Loving the wolf in sheep's clothing.
She knew the wolf was incapable of the love
The love she thought she deserved.
Still she tried anyway.
Lighting a match to a flame that had already burned
    out
It never burns quite the same, *girl*.
Girl.

The holidays come and go.
Bomb unleashed.
Boom. My entire world disrupted.

Hollow girl now stood
A stranger to her own identity
For she traded it in years ago to be a part of him
A part of *him* and for what?
She stood a shadow to his being
Only to be tossed aside and placed on a shelf.
Never first, always second or even third.
Girl.
Didn't you listen to a single thing your mom taught
    you?
No. She drank every chance she got.
Drowned herself in work
Starved herself, body and soul
A failed effort to maintain control.

"Hollow Girl"
Jessica Collazo

"you are different though;
not like these other men I know"

I sit and wonder why me?
why was I chosen out of your array of different
      women?
what is so fascinating about my melancholy madness?
is it the way I can make sweet love so insane to you
that it feels sane?
or is it the way that my body has been exposed to
      such damage since I was 15
that you can smell the scent of vulnerability and
      isolation coming from me?
you are different though;
not like these other men I know
who couldn't even tell they were making love to a
      corpse.
I was dead inside.
I buried my hatred deep inside
along with the pain I felt within me...

so deep my soul felt the imprisonment.
shackles and cuffs tied the little girl
in the forest of ruins,
lost in the whirlwinds of hopelessness
she never found her way out.
until you.
you revived that girl and watched her blossom into
    me.
still I wonder why?
you claim to love me
just by the way you touched me...
it was the demolition of me.
within me...
but it's so fucked up
because I am nothing.
just one of the many you had lined up.
collecting all kinds of hearts to see what you find,
swallowing them whole to feed your pride.

"Page 28"
Aly Maria

"I stare closely at the expressions in the cryptic decrepit photographs."

Tears well up as I view them side by side,
as I see a precursor and its post,
gaze upon the before and its after,
bear witness to the then and its now.

Pictures of moments with love
and then without. Not sure
where genuine emotion resides.
I stare closely at the expressions
in the cryptic decrepit photographs.
Is authenticity beneath the smile's lines
and tucked between the crow's toes?

It took four years for her to open the doors,
and four months more for them to slam shut.
He wasn't ready so he offered her facades.
She voluntarily fell for his window dressings.

Before, glee unaware of the lies
After, forced grins with eyes open wide.
Before, faith she had the truest of hearts
After, solo truth left when they did part.
Before, endless joy never known previously
After, unending sorrow known intimately.
Before, assurance that love's ocean was hers
After, the wreckage that drifted ashore.
Before, elated gazes up at the vast horizon
After, contemplative stares down subway tunnels.

He wasn't ready so he revealed his facade.
She fractured after falling for his dressings.
It took four years for her to open the doors,
and four months more for them to slam shut.

The photographic artifacts to untrained eyes
don't show drastic changes in that short time.
And archeologists can't differentiate between
her clever naivety and his foolish disguise,
but when I look at these images juxtaposed,
tears of remembrance well up in my eyes.

"Love's Artifacts"
Dara Kalima

"i had my heart and my mind as one until i met you..."

me before you...
i was me before you.
before the slightest thought of you
existed.
i walked around with a powerful essence
true beauty within me
you can sense my presence
as i walked in any room
i was always respected.
i had my heart and my mind as one
until i met you...
my one.
see, i never bothered to wonder
or wander about the way i can fall in love so steep
and yet you let me fall so deep
and insane
out of my fucking brain
so insane that i might've been sane
that is until you let me fall...
i was a free spirit high off life
living life and loving life
care free

feeling the breeze that will put everything at ease
i was sucka free.
until i met you.
now instead of wearing a smile
i hold this bottle
of whiskey to caress me late nights because you left
    me with open wounds
and i am scared that if i am sober i'll start to
    reminisce the moments where we stared
    together
at the moon.
i cried late nights
past the sunrise
and cried some more throughout the day because you
    ran away
with me.
you left me with a broken heart and a battered mind
a lost soul in this world of mine
now what am i left with?
a fragment of who i used to be?
pieces of me that you left me with?
to clean up the mess you made of me?
of course.
because nobody ever wants to stay after the damage is
    done.

"Page 29"
Aly Maria

"...I was god,
Your life was in my hands."

How could you put me through that?
How dare you ask me to choose?
With the weight of an ultimatum?
When in the end you ultimately lose?

Down on your knees you pleaded.
Eyes filled with sorrow,
You looked so defeated.
And yes, I took you back.
Because I was god,
Your life was in my hands.
My 16-year-old hands...

I had no fuckin' choice.
Don't you remember?
Your next breath was a decision that I had to make...
Allow me to be the cause for your funeral and wake?
I could never live with that kind of weight.

So, I took you back.
I fuckin' took you back.
And you led me down a path,
On the brink of emotional heart attacks.

Don't you remember?
You lived in anger and sadness.
And after 5 years I had to break free.
I had to cherish myself and protect my sanity.
I tried to give you the best of me,
But I was a beautiful spirit that you never could see.

"In My Hands"
Cheree Alexander-Velez

"...you hid your face
Draped in the skin of a stranger,
Another man"

Strangers never speak but speak volumes
When you won't tell me why you hurt me
Pain becomes silence, became strangers

I hurt you
Words strangle my closed throat
Like your hands gripped around my neck
Masochism finds silver lining because then at least
    you'd be touching me
Suffocating words like
"Talk to me"
"Tell me I'm special"
"Tell me I mean more to you than I could ever mean
    to her"
Her who tells me I'm special...

I hurt you
I gave away everything about me that made me special
So you hid your face
Draped in the skin of a stranger,
Another man
A man who told you that you make him feel special
A stranger who blindsided me in the dark of night
Together you buried me in hammering fists
Spattering my blood on knuckles attached to a face I
    never knew
And a face I no longer recognize

I hurt
I didn't know how to tell you what I needed
So you needed to betray me with the same knives I
    sunk into you

I felt them in my back but convinced myself I put them there
I never questioned your fidelity despite your disrespect of me
So I never knew

Never knew why you hurt me
Never knew how deep the wounds go
Never knew that as I stitched my cuts with a spool threaded of mistress seamstresses relieving seen stresses
You were unseen doing the same thing sewing the same inseam
Walking miles with my pants on fire

You were a liar
We were liars
Now I tire of lying awake at night
Fearing that the next best thing in my life
Will just be a liar too

But I will speak to her
My next best thing
I will tell her what I need from her
I will tell her that she makes me feel special

I will speak to her
When I stop being afraid of strangers
Who never speak
But speak volumes

"When Strangers Speak"
Anubis

"Did you have to suck

The sweet marrow

From my bones"

Is it not enough
That even when I was
Permitted to be
Beside you
I felt bothersome and ignored
Unwelcome little ghost girl
But now that you've run
And abandoned me
In the past
With your secrets
I know it is because I
Am wrong

Fundamentally, somehow
I am inadequate and
I don't quite fit
Is it not enough
That I always knew
I was deficient
Did you have to suck
The sweet marrow
From my bones
Gorge yourself
On the taste
Until you spit me out, alone
All too easily replaced
Is it not enough
That I am forgotten
Because I
Was never enough?

"Ghost Girl"
Luna Brasa

"Your love for me was always in misalignment."

You ever wake up from a deep sleep with a
 premonition?
Something akin to being trapped in isolation,
With your own thoughts and visions,
Of your soul's demolition.

I think I once seen mine.
I was locked in a race against time,
Losing my mind,
As my soul lifted into the air, leaving my body
 behind.

I was just a corpse on the ground.
Now a spirit unbound,
I sift through the damage as I look around,
Only to find your selfish heart...
Siphoning mine in the background.

I wanted to give you the world.
You wanted material fulfillment.
My love for you was always transferred.
Your love for me was always in misalignment.
Being open with each other was what I urged,
But your heart built its own self imprisonment.

My premonition had came true on the day that I met
    you
And looking back on it, I just had no clue,
Giving into hatred was something my mind wanted to
    do,
But deep inside I just knew it was something that I
    couldn't go through.

So I forgave and forgot,
Rewrote the ending to the plot.
Built a new me from the ruins,
And gave love another shot...

"Premonition"
Kevin P.

"I used to know a 'Me'
Whom you did not."

I used to know a 'Me'
Who did not know her identity.
She was made from the rocks you threw at her;
She was a jigsaw refusing to be pieced together.

I used to know a 'Me'
Whom you did not.
You held on to all of her heart,
Embedded it with loathing,
And self-doubt,
And stormed out.

I used to know a 'Me'
So desperate for your validation.
Drowning in someone else's skin,
Naively counting her sins,
Trying to find an ounce of proof,
That would justify the arrival of you.

I used to know a 'Me'
Who worshiped your claws.
Oblivious to the grooming,
Restricting her blooming,
Locking up her heart,
And throwing away the key.

That 'Me',
I am 'She'.
I have found the key...
And I used it to unlock,
Who I was really meant to be.

'She' is wildly kind,
Undoubtedly pure;
Free from your poisonous soul.
'She' doesn't wear masks,
Or hide from herself anymore,
Instead, breaks boundaries,
And builds her own open doors.

'She' is authentic and human,
More than you had ever been,
And distinctively mature,
Oh wait. You don't know what that means.

'She' is true to her heart,
The one she fixed on her own,
Ridding it from your chains,
And unnecessary comfort zone.

'She' is here to stay,
Unafraid and whole again,
Dancing on the corpse of 'Me',
Celebrating our victory.

"When 'Me' Met 'She'"
Nupur Nair

"you are a disease more like Eczema, Herpes, and HIV."

For some things there is a cure,
or at least a vaccination to
keep disease away,
like the flu,
or the chickenpox,
or shingles.
Some things don't need a cure
because they eventually
just fade away
like the common cold
and HPV,
but you,
you are a disease
more like Eczema,
Herpes, and HIV.
The best I can hope for
is for the symptoms
to be abated,
but I know
it would only be temporary
because there is no cure.
See, my immune system
was compromised from
the moment I was born,
and in knowing this
you keep finding your way
into my vulnerabilities,
creating flare-ups that
just bring me distress.
Fuck,
you just make me
so stressed and depressed.
I've thought of
cutting you out of my veins

like a permanent bloodletting,
but the way my fear of pain works,
that just didn't seem practical,
and then I thought about
sleeping it away.
A full bottle of
forced sleep
would do just fine
but then I thought of those
that would find me, oh
how much they would mourn
and well, even if
I don't feel all that well you,
you can't get me to drowsily
crumble under your spell,
under the influence
of your infection.
I may be immuno-compromised
but my white blood cells
are ready to fight back,
my platelets are ready to
work overtime,
in overdrive,
to fight you off every time you
insidiously attack.
Every time you keep trying,
they will,
I will
keep fighting,
even if there may be no cure.
I may be genetically predisposed,
inheriting my progenitor's
faulty parts and sensitivities
but you can't win and I,
I will do everything
to keep you at bay
even if not completely away.

"The Cure: Me"
Dara Kalima

"I am you
Not you then but you now"

Hey You
Yeah You
Can I talk to you for a second
I have to tell you it's about so real you can bet on it
You are unprepared but that'll be what sets you up
    perfectly
You will make it through most certainly
But
You are about to fall in love with a man who will
    disregard your heart so mercilessly
That you will have to heal yourself forcefully
Now before I continue with this speech that goes on
    so morbidly
Let me introduce you to myself cordially
I am you
Not you then but you now
Fully equipped with knowledge of what's about to
    happen
Fully aware of your insecurities and why this
    heartache will affect you so much back then
I am you when
I am you when you were uncomfortable with being
    yourself

When you craved to be anyone else or just someone else
I am warning you about this heartache I have already felt
But you
You have yet to go through it and unfortunately it can't be repelled
Because it makes you it doesn't break you
It pushes you past your preplanned eternity
It pushes you so far you land smack dab in your infinity
Left alone without your infantry
Where you are by yourself so you are your own enemy
Where there is no being left in your space so you have to look yourself face to face and only deal with the inner me
But I'm just speaking to you who is me
Who is naïve to the things that have yet to be
And craving for a love to come to me
Although unbeknownst to me this love will end in tragedy
And although you will temporarily admit defeat your conceit won't be written in concrete
You'll come back fighting ready to claim victory
Now I can tell you no more
But this is from me to the updated version of me
Who I'm telling you you'll adore.

"Me To Me"
Meka J. Woods

"I mourn over us the same way I mourn over my aborted child on Mother's Day"

Our relationship has become a trigger for me,
Now I bleed on these pages with a pack of sharpened
    pencils like a pack of cigarettes
I regret letting us go and I don't know if I'll ever be
    able to come back from this
In past relationships, the bad always outweighed the
    good
So when it came time to let go, I would remember all
    of the bad in order to induce the pain and gain
    the strength to never look back
I grew stronger and wiser from those experiences
When it comes to us, the good outweighs the bad and
    the sweet memories birthed from our love is
    what makes the tears fall from my eyes like
    heavy rain
No matter how much we try to separate from each
    other, our love was stronger than anything I've
    ever experienced before
Words of hatred and disrespect never left our lips
    when faced with opposition
I don't understand intuition and Spirit sometimes
To have let you go feels criminalizing
A crime of imprisonment of the heart
Perhaps from my past mistakes

They've done damage to the way I process loss and sorrow
I mourn over us the same way I mourn over my aborted child on Mother's Day
The demolition of my baby left me as a childless mother
My womb became a valley of ruins and I've been clawing my way through that clutter like a lifeless corpse for ten years
When we were together, my inner child bonded with yours and it felt like forever
Now it feels like I failed two children that I was responsible for loving and caring for
I am tortured with the thoughts of what could have been
Some might say that there must be something wrong with my brain for comparing the two levels of pain, but they are both Love in its truest forms and I've torn my heart apart from it
However, I must be insane to still believe in love
Healing is in order, especially in a time of mass isolation
So in honor of all my losses and lessons learned, I owe it to me to heal and find the love that is meant for me
But until then, I have to allow myself to grieve and bleed on these pages until this pain no longer cripples me

"Demolished Love"
Latonica Readdy

"Diminutive differences diminished our love"

Let me tell you a short story
about my first girlfriend
We were in the fourth grade
no baby teeth—almost 10

Lasted 'til fifth period
that was lunch time then
Started with a yes or no or maybe
recess it would end

Her name was Maxine
this is where I'd say how sweet
Except this story ends with me
like bubblicious under feet

Michael told me to ask her out
but Michael liked her too
Which is important to this tale
within a line or two

MAXINE FOUND OUT MICHAEL LIKED HER TOO
AND BROKE UP WITH ME BECAUSE HE WAS
TALLER

The End
...

That was so belittling
makes sense since I be little
I got short changed and pigeonholed
like monkeys in the middle

Overlooked and overshadowed
He's 4'6.2
So what? Who cares if he was taller
by an inch or 12?

(So what if that line didn't rhyme? Get over it!)

(...just like I had to get over Maxine.)

(...Which I clearly have.)
(Now, where was I?)...

something something something something
...by an inch or 12

Diminutive differences
diminished our love
least my cards were on the table...

...that I couldn't see above

        "A Short Story"

"A Short Story"
Anubis

"...you haven't yet met a mage like me

Whose chemistry isn't charmed"

You are the nature of the Universe
As far as we're concerned
But you haven't yet met a mage like me
Whose chemistry isn't charmed

Your tricks have been received by me
And I've got a plan, you see
To take back the allotted time
While creating a legacy

Our futures might be meant to cross,
And when they do you'll know---
As stars guide these gifted days
Towards answers yet unknown

"DNA"
Sarrah Safi

"...blinded by a love I thought we had So I never noticed the change"

Strolling down memory lane,
I remember when life was like a video game
I was simply on a journey through the world of
    Pokemon
Traveling as a young caterpie seeking out love and
    passion
But I was always a shy young guy
So I'd always curl up into a corner whenever a
    potential partner would come by

It wasn't until the day I met you
That confidence in myself, would spring on out the
    blue
You was a weedle locked within a self-built wall
A protective barrier hardened by a withdrawal...
...Of love
It took me some time, but I eventually softened that
    wall
Showering you with affection 'til your fears began to
    fall
And for a while this connection we had began to
    establish
Became the liberator for all our prior baggage
Until the day you presented me with a challenge
As the love we had built up together was slowly
    starting to vanish

I was blinded by a love I thought we had
So I never noticed the change
Your heart abruptly became ironclad
As your love for me began to disengage
It wasn't until the day you told me that you had
    cheated

That my high on love became just a little bit,
    complicated
I forgave you, but my affection toward you had
    progressively deflated
I tried to establish more with you, but my heart
    wasn't as motivated
And after some time I got over it, but you then
    decided to make things
Even more complicated...

It was when you started seeing an old "friend"
Resulting in more of our time together, that you'd
    often suspend
I was always suspicious as to what was going on at
    the time
But it wasn't until our eventual breakup, that light
    would shine bright on the crime
It was no more than a week after our disconnection
When you established a more familiar connection
This had sparked a fairly negative change within me
Evolving into a metapod that wanted to be cocooned
    from reality
I felt defeated, and severely broken...

This pain unfortunately would travel with me
Becoming the crack in my armor as I tried to
    continue my journey
But much like all wounds, it would heal eventually
And I'd then begin to sprout my wings, and transform
    into a butterfree
A butterfree that now lives better free
From all the pain suffered from what I now view as
    just a memory...

"A Bitter Memory"
Kevin P.

"We were left shattered like glass.

Our scars mirrored our past."

We were both led on,
Like a pencil in the hands of an inspired poet,
Writing full speed ahead & high off new beginnings!

Our relationship, like a new poem,
Open mic slot.
We were high off adrenaline,
Until that writer's block.

Trauma flooded in, like a juggernaut,
Shooting daggers,
Couldn't avoid the mental gunshots.
Our relationships were broken like the tips of pencils,
But only now do we understand the point.

We were left shattered like glass.
Our scars mirrored our past.
But after inward inspection,
We have come to recognize our own self-reflections.

"Hard Truth"
Cheree Alexander-Velez

> "Both exchange energies
> His negativity contaminated for positivity."

Falling for his one last conversation
Changing NADA!
Giving him opportunity to feed her
More emptiness and BULLSHIT!
Filling her cup with poison
Contaminating her insides with his bacteria

Beneath her anger was fear
Feeling life isn't fair
Happiness is a choice
Everything temporary
Less is more

All she needed was a little
Affection, appreciation and attention
His words didn't match his actions
Good at talking
Terrible at supporting

He knew exactly what he was doing to her
He didn't give two fucks
Selfish and ignorant
Okay with losing her
No regret controlling her thoughts

Both exchanged energies
His negativity contaminated her positivity
He carried guilt, shame and past trauma
Open wounds and infected scars
Corrupted files downloaded within each embrace

Changed behavior she prayed for
She wasn't his only choice, but he was hers
His ignorance taught her how to let go
He basked in her suffering
She rejoiced through her adjusting

Forgave him for things, he would've hated and left
    her for
Took her forgiveness and love for granted
Pain made her stronger
Tears made her braver
Heartbreak made her wiser and grateful for it all

Body wanted sex
Heart yearned love
Soul needed peace
He wasn't expecting her to change direction
No longer seeking to compromise

Growth through pain
Emotionally deleted him
Healing all the disgrace
One day he will ache in regret
Truth will hit

Like a mountain crumbling
Only then he'll realize
How he was destroying her
Setting fire to his infectious treatments
Giving birth to a new life of self-care and self-worth

Seeking someone to kiss her wounds
Celebrate her scars
Accept her imperfections
Understand the past is the past
Accepting her as she is

Someone who will make love to her soul
She did see him once again
Teaching a workshop
Told everyone to look up mental illnesses
His picture came up first

Only reason he misses her
She looks amazing
Doing extremely well
Still single after a year
Left no open avenues for any connection
Tables turn
Feeling the emptiness, he once inflicted
Depression and anxiety
Visits frequently
Loneliness moving in

Constant panic attacks
Loss of appetite
No incentive to do shit
Karma took its course
Everything began to hit

"Watering A Dead Rose"
Keisha Molby-Baez

"...you coddled this Frankenstein heart..."

Like a shattered mirror
a broken heart still functions—
loving in shards and distorted reflections.
This defective heart always gave
everything that was demanded—
loyalty, obedience, silence.
It always sought unhealthy attention.
Sifting through memories archived long ago—

love was always: compliance, desperation, discomfort,
         touching, do not speak.
But you coddled this Frankenstein heart
and taught it that broken is okay.
Love is not demanding and does not strip away.
Love is equivalent and replenishing.
Love can be deep and unconditional.
A broken heart can still learn
to love mended with scars.

"Untitled 7"
Lea Elani

REFLECTION

"The only thing that possess both the problem and the solution is found in your mirror."

"...waiting for my demolition as I slowly bleed from the inside out."

The damage was done way before I could even comprehend the depths of isolation my soul would feel. Imprisoned by my own mind, filled with hatred and pain. Outside forces preying on my innocence, waiting for my demolition as I slowly bleed from the inside out.

I was left in ruins, only my corpse remained. Going insane trying to figure out who's in control of such a dirty game of give and take. Asking myself, "Lord, why did you have to do me this way?"

"Untitled 8"
LaDasha-Diamond

"Let me pour us some drinks

A toast to destruction..."

Hatred will bring
The demolition of my life
A corpse that I carry
Around my throat
A testament to the damage done
Rather than free myself from
The weight of this imprisonment
I choose isolation
My hollow heartbeats
Keeping company with these ruins

You might call me insane
Let me pour us some drinks
A toast to destruction
An ode to self-damnation
Maybe the cups all have poison
Maybe I drink
Maybe I die alone here
Does it matter anyway?
Cheers.

"An Ode To Self-Damnation"
Luna Brasa

"She picked a new colour,
One from the seven in a rainbow…"

I refuse to call it trauma.
For my body swallowed it,
Much before my soul did.

You see, bathing a brown girl in foundation,
While tenderly seven and innocently driven.
It kills the sparkle in her eyes,
It makes her question if Jasmine was the one,
Meant to be hidden and imprisoned in that lamp.
Because surely blue is better than brown.

At seven, she hadn't learned to swim yet,
Fearing the marks that the water would leave,
Because she could bleach but not tan,
This was strictly the ban,
In a home surrounded by seven deserts.

If she were gifted all her seven lives,
She would skip this one;
She would rather be burned than returned to that day.
But they stayed. The foundations.
Now accompanied by fairness creams,
Scrubs, packs, concealers…
Anything that would stick to her,
Better than this face.

One day however,
She picked a new colour,
One from the seven in a rainbow,
She would hold on to a new one each day;
The seven days felt more magical that way.
For she could be unseen with some green,
Or borrow a bit of blue to pull her through.

That little girl had some magic up her sleeves,
It carried her across the seven seas,
To discover that maybe,
Brown is not all she was meant to be,

Beautiful comes along with it involuntarily.

"SEVEN"
Nupur Nair

"It's time for you to expand your aura

And improve what you can procure…"

Dear Magnificent Soul
Your tears are not shed in vain
They act as guiding rivers
Carrying action through your pain
You are needed in this era
With everything you've ever endured

It's time for you to expand your aura
And improve what you can procure
These happenings were never random
Your world's transforming somehow
You're never alone on your journey
You're where you're needed right now

"To: You"
Sarrah Safi

"Each day I live with the collateral damage."

When the sun sets, I get upset.
Because in creeps that demon of my past,
A corpse that hasn't died yet.

Each day I live with the collateral damage.
As isolation chokes me,
Hatred provokes me,
Fear over the years,
Has officially broken me.

I try to build bricks of bravery,
But I'm stuck in a mental slavery,
Of imprisonment.

Paranoia settles deep in my brain
Am I going insane?
My courage turns to debris, like ruins,
And explodes like a grenade!

But I keep looking over my shoulder...
Should I be this afraid?

"When the sun sets"
Cheree Alexander-Velez

"The hatred lingers like a corpse, driving me insane..."

I've not yet discarded the corpse of this hatred
It lingers in my isolation
I long to be free of its influence
But I'm unsure of its demolition...

Do I forgive it for my imprisonment?
When it stole my freedom from me?
When it stole my love and my trust
From the world I was meant to see?

No,
I refuse to play the victim
In this insane charade of thought
Within its damage lies the ruins
Of a slowly dying heart

Still...

The hatred lingers like a corpse, driving me insane,
The damage I've encountered is seemingly in vain
I stand in bitter ruins of this isolation
I'm with the zombie of a former self
Feeding hungrily at my brain---
Mocking my imprisonment
As demolition reigns

"Zombie"
Sarrah Safi

"A pile up of trauma
Buried under trauma…"

9:13pm trauma
No one knows my name
Doctors surrounding in panic
Inquisitive to what had happened
Reading my anatomy
Close to flat line
Incoming call from my parents
Attempting to find me
Nurse holds my slightly, blue cold hands
Heart falls still in time

Shocks to my chest
Eyes open with fear
Feeling lost and displaced
Trying to leave my trauma in prayers
Hands to my chest
Pains so heavy
My soul is beginning to flatten
Attempting to join my soul back with my body
Full body trauma
13 hours in ICU

Pain engulfing my spirit
Trapped in a cocoon of horror
The sight of my mother
Allowed hope to creep back in
Doctors revisit my room
24 hours passed
It is 9:13pm again
An evil violation revealed
A vessel
Carries the blackness of my aches

Thoughts turn to ashes
Clips of what occurred
Strapped into a go-kart
No brakes, 30 miles per hour
13 go-karts behind me
The most deafening crash
The curtains to my eyes immediately closed
Explanation of crash
Stomach bent steering wheel
Go-kart disassembled

Organs displaced
Head trauma
Swollen and bruised all over
Demons tried to possess me
Parents traumatized
Pondering how their 13-year-old will digest this
Depression eats away
I am young and innocent
Reflecting on depression's deadly grasp
Most difficult part

Finding myself again
I was only 13 and battling mentally
Sleepless nights
Depression the anxiety
Trauma the depression
Trauma linked to my womb
My trauma refused to follow
Rules of flesh and bone
Buried deep within my recesses
Becoming a part of me

Trying to tend to my trauma
Patience and tenderness necessary
Trauma just lingers
Building a home
Stomach twisting horror
Ripped from ever being a mother
Trauma fills me
My head and chest
Arms and fingers
Moving through my body

Expanding and engulfing everything
Using every nerve to fight for energy
Black hole building
Stuck in a state of darkness
Head pitch black
Tears and anxiety trap me
Climbing up my esophagus
Clogging my throat
Suffocating my happiness
Blocking my airway

I never told anyone I was depressed
Nor suffering with anxiety
Afraid of being judged and labeled broken
This trauma crawls through my head like worms
Eating away at my positive thoughts
A demon I let in
Through one word, "NEVER"
Flashbacks cutting deep
Feeling the crash over and over
Visions consume me

Neglecting my deep emotions
Struggling with the thought of never
Being able to bear a child
Tremendous pain
Leaving an invisible stain
Through an unfortunate accident
Wounding my spirit
Realizing trauma has no limits
It triggers fear
Fear of driving

Fear of being in a vehicle
Trauma is a voice
I should've never got in
Trauma watches me
What I do and don't do
Screaming at myself
Wishing it were a different outcome
Begging it never happened
Trauma is the hole I keep
One that I find myself in year after year

Trauma is debilitating
Repeated openings of the same wound
Only to hit a dead end every time
Watching my course change
Trauma is a voice
I am fine
No one can tell me I'm not
This was my best kept secrct
The worst accident ever
Two deep and unable to fix

A pile up of trauma
Buried under trauma
I'm full of darkness
Mind sick
Filled with built up hate and anger
Inescapable sadness
13 visions consistently
Waking up each time drenched in horror
Constant lumps of anxiety in my throat
Is there anything worse?

Starving myself of hope and a miracle
Often repressed
Feelings remain but less
Seven years later, it's 9:13pm and we meet again
Best friends we are
Falling in love
Holding in eighty percent of me
Terrified to inform him
About what was taken from me
At the age of 13

Fighting with my inner self
Scared to reveal it all
What could destroy our union
Will he still love me?
No longer able to nurture
A seed inside of me
Riddled with trauma
He smiles and says, "no worries"
We are one and the same
Tell me how you came to be

He was born unable to release potent sperm
His tears began to leak
From his light, brown puppy eyes
Is there anything worse?
Stop blaming yourself
This was none of God's doing
Watch and see
How he will bless you and me
Health and strength all we ask
Something changes

Something snaps
Part of me dies
Hideous parts bloom
I'm not all damaged goods
This trauma doesn't seal my fate
Reconnecting mind, body and soul
Reclaiming the 13-year-old it stole
Two years later
The power of blessings
Evident inside of me

Three months in
No signs
High risk it is
Atopic condition
Extreme strength begun
C-section planned
Trauma tried to revisit
Again, on January 24, 2000
Blood running down my legs
Eyesight ripped from me

Hearing escaped me too
Pleading for the life inside of me
Repeating, "just take me"
Devil tries to revisit
Again at 9:13pm
Praying trauma does not settle in
Both heartbeats stopped for 13 minutes
Bright light trying to creep in
Both our eyes open
Curtain over me

Body cold and aching
Waiting for confirmation
Yearning to hear that sound
The most precious cry
13 seconds later
Gratitude sunk in
We're both alive
Yes!
I win!
Trauma wasn't able to revisit again

"Suddenly"
Keisha Molby-Baez

"Pain laid into me like my hand was on a stove…"

The first thing to break was my heart
After I thought it was a true work of art
The next thing to fall apart was my mind
It got so bad that I was impossible to find
She placed my heart into the meat grinder
As if physical pain wasn't a clear reminder

(so I thought would I ever be able to feel)

This is when I was introduced to a new friend
By some people I knew rather well in a way
There was Sadness who brought along Regret
And then Depression came back with Anxiety
There were new ones like Rage Blame & Hate
They also managed to bring along Madness
The new four I was never truly fond of before

(this is in no way my life it can't be real)

Pain laid into me like my hand was on a stove
Cutting into me like a hot knife through butter
Blame brought up old things that happened
To make me somewhat feel bad for this issue
Rage had the tendency to force me to tears
By bringing up all of my past failures in life
Madness was one who was a total nutcase
He often talked of Death as a way out of this
There was one who called himself Creativity
He introduced me to a viable solution to this
Then I was blessed with a notebook and pen

(my emotions just continue to mess with me)

In reality my life wasn't getting any better
I finally decided to just write a simple letter
This so called "letter" wasn't that after all
I never expected to be able to stand up tall
This was my first heartfelt poem "BROKEN"
It was so hard but I was glad to be outspoken

(Creativity opened my eyes and now I can see)

"The Heartbreak"
Mike Cruz

> "My existence is of light and shadow
> And the shades of in-between…"

It is a maddening time
When my ghosts come back to haunt me
They live in my ravaged thoughts and blood
The hormones that hang the heart heavy

Pulses
Of Worry
Pulses
Of Hate
Pulses that send my heart
Pleading for break

I'm stuck with these obscure emotions
Conjured from insanity
A PTSD version of
A deluded reality

But as I watch my demons play
As night's clock blinks 3:33
The flashing trigger sends my mind astray
With the ghosts I no longer contain

They might be in my memories
There's no doubt they're in my blood
But I control their influence
In my actions and my love

My existence is of light and shadow
And the shades of in-between
Pulling my mind to balance
Is an action, not a dream

It is only upon this realization,
The ghosts begin to fade
The demons become quiet
And for a moment, time's unmade

I fill this void with comprehension
I fill it with understanding
The ghosts of the past were never enemies
They brought meaning to a story worth telling

"Thank You , Ghosts"
Sarrah Safi

"that joy thief, Comparison..."

I know how ephemeral allure is in the Western world.
Still,
bombarded by the simony
of the black female body---
tapered waist
two ripe peaches sitting at 90 degrees above/below
a belly flat as newly laid flooring--
that joy thief,
Comparison,
sneaks in.
Got me hearing,
feeling the gaze of my ex affixed to passing a brown
      beauty.
He named her Stallion.

Sometimes I look in the mirror and not seeing that
      idoneous image,
my face descends into a moue.
A chyron of erstwhile childhood taunts runs through
      my chockablock mind.
Nostalgia for the breviloquent street corner
      compliments that came more often in my youth.
Sometimes I be ducking invitations for photos
fearing macabre lighting revealing uncomeliness.
Find myself too busy for an open mic
that my voice, that stills tumultuous rooms,
will appear amateur amongst the performers
who stir the stomping shouting snapping.

But the ever-flowing waterfalls of love and care
God and Goddess
my grandparents
mother and father
aunts uncles cousins sister son niece my man
sistergirls and brotherfriends
have poured into me
always rejuvenate.

I rax.
Remember beauty ain't no solo act.
Diamonds
Rubies
Emeralds
Opals
Pearls.

"Memorandum"
Carla M. Cherry

> "Purging my soul
>
> Focusing on inner strength..."

Anyone there?
Can you hear me knocking?
Presence of an angel
Soft voice repeating
"I'm here to save you"
No answer
She can't hear a frequency that low
You prayed for me
Why can't you hear me?

Enduring so much
Excruciating pain
A killer disease
Trying to leave me insane
Feeling like I'm dying
Determined I had to be
A parasite it was

Leaving a pile of shattered emotions
Struggling to break away from it
My suffering
My struggles
My pain was messengers
Carrying my remedy all along
All I had to do
Feel it deep within me
Suffering was a gift

Teaching me mind over matter
Hidden mercy I found
A remedy in pain
Focus on love
Focus on helping
Focus on achieving
Focus on creating

Focus on forgiveness
My pains gave birth to extended life
Finding barriers within it
Breaking each down, one by one
Pain her greatest alley
Searching for a cure
Learned to not expect
Only demand respect
Strength unfolding

Looking to the Heavens
Hope I see
No matter what happens
I always love me
Knocked down by horrid symptoms
Standing tall with confidence
Lessons learning

Continuing to move forward
Brings great reward
Mental and physical growth
Pain into purpose poetry
Therapy within her story
Purging my soul
Focusing on inner strength
When it flows consistently
I welcome it with open arms

Recognizing it
Creating a healing connection
Placed me in a cocoon before
Now I'm transforming
Many deep wounds it left
Sweet words sealed them up
My attempt to survive

Releasing the power within it
All along lying dormant
Embraced my darkness
Registering it as pleasure
Found hidden blessings
Within each inflicted wound
Taking nothing in vain
Unbelievable, how remedy
Derived from pain.

"The Cure"
Keisha Molby-Baez

"...Eccentric souls daringly ink pain into poetry hoping to find relief..."

Perfect strangers sounds too cliché for this meeting of hearts
A mutual inner standing of pain connected them from the start
A deep sense of knowing, conversation uninterrupted despite deep breaths
Inhaling new ways of being and exhaling the suffered abuse
No loner I but we another duo quoting #metoo

Standing in solidarity for a world violent free
Pain can be tricky and sometimes unseen
But these eccentric souls daringly ink pain into
    poetry hoping to find relief
No longer victims but thriving survivors rewriting the
    narrative of their so-called traumatic lives,
    triumphantly.

"Untitled 9"
LaDasha-Diamond

"Risen from the dead
Again and again..."

Today, I am letting you go.
It's been years and I'm tired of playing tag with my
    past.
Spice Girl stickers adorn those photo albums
Hiding the hurt I've been carrying for all this time.
Mami pulled out the photo albums the other day
And that small insecure girl I saw is no longer here.
She's pulled through the trenches,
Risen from the dead
Again and again,
A woman.

And now I stand.
The shame from years of self hate and degradation,
The constant comments about my body,
My body,
How it wasn't a suitable thing to look at,
It wasn't the proper home for love.
Love. Only love I was missing was my own.

This is MY body. You only get one
And I am done carrying the past pain on my back.
I'm packing it tight.
It's time to make things right with me.
No more time to bleed.

"Today"
Jessica Collazo

"Taken ambivalently
Joy and fear flooding simultaneously..."

Ladder
Assured victory framed within 4 bars
Splinters sanded down and honey coated over
As if the death of the mighty mahogany was not enough

Each step onto the dead
Driving me forward towards my place on which to
    imitate it
Just 4 feet above my head
Looking up
Felt like 4 miles
Looking down

With step 1
I am ensured the ladder is real
Faith fails me as it offers no security

But step 2
Is proof that the ladder would hold my weight
As I wait to reach the top
I have determined not to stop until I reach the loft
And the pillow that awaits me

And step 3
Taken ambivalently
Joy and fear flooding simultaneously
I can see beyond what my eyes can see at eye level
I level my body for the final step

And then
Darkness

My eyes open
I look up
Neck bent
Feet erect above my head
My head against the wall at the foot of my ladder
Disoriented

Up is down and down is up
Feels like forever before feeling returns
In a manifestation of a pain sensation in my head
My neck
My head

Wailing escapes my angled throat as I hope for a
    savior above to absolve me of my failing

Just 4 feet above my head
And it occurs to me
I have fallen off the ladder to the top of my bed

"Ladder"
Anubis

"Succumbing from the inside, Deliberating for dreams to coincide."

I was sweetly naive, who was trying to survive.
People thought I spoke less, but they didn't know I was reckless.
Succumbing from the inside, deliberating for dreams to coincide.
Doing things to please people, committing unconsciously, infractions ample.
Was so deep inside that I was lost in the darkness of being successful at any cost.
Thought everybody can be friend, nothing could be untrusted.
Watching over the shoulders of people who were backbitchers clipping staple.
Roasting my nature making fun of the character.
That was the time I was hurt like my burning heart was ignited with the sacks of coal.
Passing juncture I realised I was meant to be the same way I was.

But the reality is a bitch, she made a snitch, made me
    do things that I could never stitch.
I made myself a whole new bastard self-loathing in
    ego and people pleaser,
Dunked inside the lake of blind faith and
    overconfidence wait it's just a teaser.
I overcame the fears of being in the corner in the dark
    by myself,
But by the time I realised I wasn't that old myself.
Things changed people too, circumstances changed
    fates too, I did whatever it was in my hand to
    do.
Now as you can see, I'm crying loud through this inks
    on my papers,
Trying to compensate with myself full of errors.
Hope you don't mind watching me saddened in my
    saltwater, I am swimming in every aspect
    of position to get out from underwater.

"Reality Is Bitch"
Dhruvil Purani

"Reality knocks the wind out of my chest every time..."

Self-neglect and complacency creeps through the
 cracks in my smile these days
Reality knocks the wind out of my chest every time I
 realize that I'm alone again
I could fill all the droughts with my tears and still feel
 like I'm drowning in my existence

I thought forever meant forever but that's not the case
 for me
It feels like I can never look at love in the face the
 same way ever again
Lover's PTSD has got a hold on me stronger than the
 powers that be

These days, I curl up in my bed knees to chest
    weeping
When asked, I say that I'm okay knowing that I have a
    gaping hole in my chest
Trying to keep it together, I've become a Mrs. Hyde
    in this landfill

Hiding how ill I feel inside, I try to survive with a
    smile on my face during the daytime
Knowing that the pain of my reality will shed come
    nightfall

"Mrs. Hyde's Dark Valley"
Latonica Readdy

"The result of your reoccurring pain is a corpse"

Over time your actions led to your demolition
You'd ignore feelings of self-hatred for years
All the negative thoughts drove you insane
These actions lead you to self-imprisonment
Bad decisions have placed you on this road

It brings you to a mountain hidden in the ruins
You think this is of course the perfect isolation
Because finally this is where you can meditate
But you come to realize that you are not alone
In this place that you are able call as your own
An ideal metaphor for all the self-inflicted pain

You see a few distinct versions of who you are
The result of your reoccurring pain is a corpse
The self-pain has drove you to physical pain
Scars will serve as a reminder of the damage
But the wounds that hurt most you won't see...

"Bad Perspectives"
Mike Cruz

"My pores exhale the scent of lemons around me like an invisible halo."

I had let myself be convinced that what God has made
    must be tamed.
17 years of blow dryers.
Pigtails. Plaits. Cornrows. Hot combs. Three perms.
At 19, I began to love the bend and curves of my own
    hair.
Afros. Twists.
But hair that hung straight got the most oohs and aahs.
Hours of blending synthetic fibers into braids
for the illusion of long tresses, hours untangling them.
Began to admire locs but was scared
of growing my hair into such a permanent state.
Wouldn't be able to sometimes straighten my hair for
    the oohs, the aahs.
When I turned 40, I met a sister with bountiful,
    beautiful kinky curls.
She arranged my kinks into twists that adorned my
    face.
I fell in love with my God-given hair.
Once in a while I'd ask her to flat iron my hair, for the
    most oohs and aahs.

At 47, with a man who rolled my hair into his hands
    who exhaled oohs and aahs,
I had my stylist twist my hair into sections. Let them
    be.

Twice a month she takes my hair into her hands.
Massages peppermint shampoo into my strands, my
    scalp.
I be the shore, she be the sea.

As it dries, she caresses my hair, my scalp with
    rosemary, almond, spearmint oils.
As she gathers new growth and rolls it into the old,
we movers, shakers, mothers, teachers, entrepreneurs,
    artists
be bragging on ourselves, our men, who build,
    sometimes break our hearts,
in this space where blackness needs no defending, no
    explanation.
My locs embrace my face.
My pores exhale the scent of lemons around me like
    an invisible halo.
After wishing my sisters well, I step out into Harlem.
Every roll of my hips, my neck, a holy celebration.

"Bend"
Carla M. Cherry

HEALING

"The disease always makes way for the cure."

"Enmeshed with my identity, we became each other."

Loved to the edge of death,
you have never left me.
The obsession---consuming,
at times you were all that existed.
Etched within my ego and soul,
you scarred, a permanent memorial.
Enmeshed with my identity,
we became each other.
Guiding my choices, dictating my emotions,
I could never fathom life without you.

I wither at this crossroad,
wasted to living bones.
A whisper goodbye, tear-drenched cheeks
this journey is no longer about you.
We will meet again along this path,
an acquaintance of long lost friends.
Please don't beg, it's not a fight to be won
and I anxiously turn away.
Steps moving forward, joyful tears on my face,
you shrill, screaming out my name.
But my dear friend, pain, I do not look back
as I begin my travels alone.

"Untitled 10"
Lea Elani

"...when I finally return home, I will be sure to write."

My spine feels damaged,
From the weight of this baggage,
It has been bringing me down,
For way too long now,

So, I believe it is time.

Allow me a pit stop,
As I discard these contents,
Deliver them to their proud owners,
Granting my soul some overdue rest.

I spot a cracked mirror first,
The shards from it unable to cut me,
The way it's done before,
Dried stains of my broken self-esteem,
Line it's jagged edges.

I shatter what's left of it,
Collect the remains,
And return it to the shop of horrors.
'Puberty'

Next, I use my sore palm,
To pick up a frame marked Ex,
I dismantle the strong bolts,
With my bare hands,
The way it had once tried,
To unravel me and my spirit.

I burn its eroding photo,
And return the ashes to the ground,
Burying it deeper than,
The self-love I had once lost.

I reunited myself with the same self-love,
Wrapped it on my arm,
And continued the cleanse.

Somewhere between some lies and cheats,
I discover a heavy bottle of grief,
It was filled to the brim,
With the heaviest tears,
Reminding me of those salty scars,

Without a second thought,
I poured it down the drain,
It will be returned to space,
On its way to discovering,
A new burden to carry,
A new heart to heal.

Now my bag is almost empty,
Except for my only essential,
A rusted old key,
Whose lock I am yet to find,
So when I finally return home,
I will be sure to write.

Goodbye for now.
My soul wishes,
To take flight again.

"Goodbye"
Nupur Nair

"Deuces to the demons & Peace out to all the drama."

Farewell to the fears that fractured my mental.
Farewell to the darkness that made my body tremble.
Deuces to the demons &
Peace out to all the drama.
Adios to the adversities,
'Cause we survived through our trauma.

Deuces to the damage that my heart kept.
Adios to heartbreaks & suicide threats.
Sayonara to sadness.
Goodbye to the depression.
Now on the path to renewal & progression.

Hola to vulnerable feelings.
Hello to poetry as a beacon.
Healing resides in my heart,
I am now tasting freedom!

"Peace Out!"
Cheree Alexander-Velez

"...the darkest times can bring me to the brightest places."

If I have learned anything from life,
It is that sometimes the darkest times can bring me to
    the brightest places.
I've learned that most toxic people can teach me the
    most important lessons.
That my most unbearable struggles can grant me
    abundant necessary growth.
That the most heartbreaking losses of friendship and
    love can make room for the most wonderful
    people.
I've learned that whatever seems like a curse at the
    moment can actually be a blessing.
That what seems like the end of the road is actually
    just discovered that I was meant to travel down
    to another road.

I've learned that no matter how difficult things seem, there's always hope.
That no matter how powerless we feel or how horrible things seem I can't give up.
I have to, need to keep going.
Even when it's scary, even when all of my strength has gone, I have to pick myself back up and move forward.
Whatever I am battling at the moment, it'll pass and I'll make it through.
I've made it this far, I can make it through whatever comes next.

"Winning The Battle"
Dhruvil Purani

"I am grateful for the pain you inflicted for I would not know joy..."

Farewell I bid to you, emotional trauma.
I am grateful for the pain you inflicted for I would not know joy;
I appreciate the experience of anger an
      disappointment for I would not know self
      determination and love;

I am thankful for betrayal and deception for it taught
 me self reliance and compassion;
Through all the emotional ups and downs I am
 stronger and more resilient;
Thank you for revealing to me my purpose of
 spreading light into the darkness...and the
 ability to transform trauma into triumph!

"Untitled 11"
LaDasha-Diamond

"...my soul could never again fly in terror."

The voice of the attendant whispered softly in my ear,
"Flight 603 will be departing shortly ma'am."
As I turned to match her voice with my ears,
I took a look at the other passengers hungrily waiting
 and patiently anticipating.
One by one,
They lined up in single file.
Some had newspapers,
Some had tea,
Some had sandwiches,
And others stared ahead-blank faces deprived of
 sleep.
"Ma'am could you step forward please?"
The attendant spoke once more.
But this time, I snapped out of my reverie and daze.
Stepping back in confusion and dismay.
"I'm sorry, this is not my plane. I must've booked this
 one in error."
"No ma'am, this is Flight 603, and you're in the right
 space, so please step forward, and take your
 place."

I looked at the passengers one more time again,
And saw that they all had names:
Abandonment was some tall, brown-looking fellow,
Shame was some pink lady with orange hair and
    crooked teeth,
Mis-trust was a baby cradled in her mother's arms,
And Egg-shells sat delicately in a corner.
I picked up my carry on,
And took a deep sigh,
I stood in front of the attendant with my head high.
I told her I was leaving,
And that indeed this was not my flight,
But perhaps it was booked in error,
And that my soul could never again fly in terror.
I was destined for more, and now that I am better,
I do not have to fly with passengers reminiscent of a
    script buried and dead.
The attendant grew quiet,
As I readied myself to leave.
With a smile on my face,
And determination on my sleeve.
To never go back,
To always move forward,
I said good-bye to Flight 603,
And booked another flight to depict my new story.

"Flight 603"
Taneeka L. Wilder

"For god's sake, bleed. And bleed openly."

They say, "What doesn't kill you makes you stronger"
I don't agree, some things that didn't kill me,
Came so close that they're still deteriorating.
They didn't make me better, some made me worse.
And can't that be okay too?
Can't some things just break you?
This whole freaking world wants you to believe that
    admitting defeat makes you weak.
For god's sake, bleed. And bleed openly.
There can be pride in vulnerability.
The honesty is a kind of maturity.
And really, it's the things that did kill me, that
    made me.

You regret your deeds in context to feel guilty,
But is it worth it to let your guilt be followed
By sorrowness of own mental state.
Our past gives us our identity,
We look to the future for salvation and fulfilment.
Past is gone and can't be relived,
And this future is a mere illusion.
The essence of life is in the now,
Life is where you are at this very moment.
We must learn to slow down our minds,
In order to appreciate the vitality.
The more we focus on the past and future,
The more we miss the present.
The past is a memory and the future is anticipation,
But the present is life itself.

"Bleed Openly"
Dhruvil Purani

"With you, I was never alone
We begin and end together..."

You were a part of me
Before I even knew
How to speak
Rooted in the deepest facets
Of my being
We have walked
Through every stage together
Hand in claw
Even abandoned
With you, I was never alone
We begin and end together
Your darkness
Kept me hidden
Your claws and fangs
Kept me safe
I am not scared of you
My constant companion
If I'm being honest
We've walked so far together
I'm scared I'm nothing
Without you
I have been doubled over
For so long
I don't think these bones
Can hold me
I've kept my heart safe
In a chokehold between
These ironclad palms

I think it may crumble
At the first whisper of freedom
My skin perpetually
Encased in armor
Will burn at the slightest
Hint of sunlight
Will bleed at the mere whisper
Of attention
My pain, my protector
I wear your presence
Like a warning sign
My reflection
Who am I without you?
I fear if I pour light
Into our cracks
That I may kill us both
But, it might be worth a try
My oldest friend
It might be time for me
To walk alone
Steps shaking
Breaths bouncing
I walk us to the edge
We stare at the water below
Claws and fingers entwined
I step over the guardrail
I stop me as I try to follow
Quizzically, I look at me
Until understanding dawns
Across our face

"It's not safe." I begin.
"It never was." I counter.
"You'll get hurt." I try to tell myself.
"I think I'm supposed to. I think that's
What it's all about." I whisper, terrified.
"I have kept you safe."
"I know you have. Thank you."
"They're going to break
your heart. All of them. Every day."
"Love means I have to let them in
And trust they won't."
"Is it worth it?"
"I don't know."
Tears streaming down my face
I look back at you
All the pain I've carried
Do I dare leave you behind?
Untether you from the
Deepest parts of me
And dare to walk free
"But I think it's time to find out."
And I jump.
I fall.
I plunge.

Into the cold water
Beneath me
I hold my breath
While I am cleansed
Left defenseless
Skin too thin
Heart beating unhindered
And I wait
For the light
To find me
To fill me
For the water to wash away
These transgressions
Teach me to bend
For the earth to heal me
To claim me
For the air to teach me how
To run and laugh
Set me right
I am waiting
I am becoming
I am healing
I am trying.

"Hand in Claw"
Luna Brasa

> "Waving pain goodbye
> Bleeding it all out with a sigh"

Hey You!
Trauma hovering
Lifelong pains and suffering
Many ups and downs
Bled at each of the rounds
Insidious thing
Torment you bring
Most terrible of all
Trauma's Ball

Wounds wishing to heal
Needle-sharp memories reveal
Stomach twisting horror
Tore the best out of her
Throwing up experiences
Death rehearses
Few times almost successful
No more feeling regretful

Poetry my therapist
Painting my hobby
Praying my medicine
Writing my PCP
Different survival stories
Beautiful glories
Processing emotions
Welcoming promotions

Lingering smell of sickness
Mental illness
Evil violations
Writing my own Revelations
Unfortunate encounters
No longer my downers
Tore me apart many times
Committing multiple crimes

Killing you over and over
All the buildup drove her
Each time you visited
Darkness you distributed
No more secret passages
She becomes one of the savages
Entering mind, body, and soul
Unachievable goal

Poisoning any future attempt
You are now exempt
Old version of myself died
Reborn inside
No more constant lumps of anxiety in my throat
Good riddance I wrote
Feeding you to the wolves
Ridding this victory with bulls

Trauma doesn't last forever
Collective endeavor
Goodbye P.T.S.D.
Pain, trauma, stress and depression
Leaving the battlefield with one word, YES!
I'm truly blessed
Surviving all the trials
Lifetime of pain bottled up in vials

Decapitated you are
Heart left with an ugly scar
Quarantined and now free
Broken mended
Pain pleasure
Trauma strength
Regret released
No longer bruised and unattended

Infected your abuse
This situation I diffuse
Path of forgiveness undergoing
Graduation approaching
My life no longer tainted
Filling the ocean with tears painted
Red carpet of accomplishments laid out for me
An angel with one wing flying free

Waving pain goodbye
Bleeding it all out with a sigh
Everything bottled up inside
A final wave I ride
No more sorrows will be born
Positivity and happiness sworn
Love and gratitude fill my heart
Waving a final goodbye as I depart

"Valediction"
Keisha Molby-Baez

"I am determined to be released..."

I sat here too long,
collecting too much,
knee deep in deadly artifacts.
They don't serve me,
they bury me,
slowly killing me.
But today,
today, I toss them away.
No donation or recycle bin,
no one inherits this heap,
this treasured
painfullest-of-pains
trash heap.
Like the brown dress I wore
when meeting my rapist.
I was cute,
it was cute
but not since that moment.
I can't wear it,
yet I can't let it go,
can't let him go,
can't release myself
from the self-blame pain.
I hold tight to it,
just like her funeral program,
it anchoring me
to her cancerous finale
and not the light
my sister's existence gave.
And this,
this cigar,
dad's cigar has been
suffocating my
asthmatic lungs,
my mental health,
and my hopes and my dreams.

It's never been lit,
but I cherished it,
when it and he
couldn't cherish me.
And we can't forget
this model SUV resembling
the one my abuser trapped me in
as he told me about my inadequacies.
Then there are these piles of racial tensions
stacked as high as
the gaslit chandeliers.
And over there the dust collects
on the souvenirs from my election loss,
reminding me of my public failure
and not the personal victories.
Yes,
these piles
have been heaping for too long,
into the trash bags they must go.
They must go and
I must be,
I am determined to be released
so that I can be
uninhibited in my home,
in my heart
and in my dome.
Yes,
I have sat here,
slowly dying here,
being buried here
by these piles for way too long,
and now it's time to pack them up,
wrap them up,
and treat it all
like the trash
it always was.

"Released and Reformed"
Dara Kalima

"This was my life, simply at a prior checkpoint..."

Today is the day...
That I say goodbye to all the pain and worry
All the things that have dragged me by my feet
    for years
All the things that have laced my face with tears
As today is that day

Today is the day that I reveal the triforce
Summoning the power to control my destiny
The courage to face my reality
And the wisdom to process it all with clarity...
But it took me years to obtain these three,
As I had to first cleanse the love triangle
That was deep within me

I had to absolve myself of all the pain
And disdain obtained
When my father walked out,
Without properly passing the reins
I had to step up to the power and responsibility
That was left to support the family
Flipping that disdain into love
That will now uphold my accountability

I had the courage within oneself
To break through the barriers and isolation
That was once placed on myself
These barriers that were built up to gather
The remains of a broken heart
When a former love of mine left my heart for another
But by finding that courage within me
I was able to rise up from the rubble
And search again for the right love for me

I had to look inside myself and find new perspectives
Reflect upon my imperfections
To acquire wisdom for a new objective
This objective was to take what I use to hate about me
And learn to love myself without scrutiny
By accepting what it is that I've come to be
I can venture forward with self-love that's carefree
Allowing me to control my own power and courage directly
As I ascend through life's journey

I've gone through a multitude of experiences in my life
But today I take all that I've learned
And mesh it together with the confidence I've earned
To proceed onward without spite
Love has been the glue that's held me together up until this point
And I won't allow spite a voice to exploit
The feelings of fear that once held my heart up at gunpoint
This was my life, simply at a prior checkpoint
But I'm now saying goodbye to my former self
As I move toward a future that I can use to look back upon myself
With a smile...

"Good Riddance"
Kevin P

**"She opens the door and I drink her in.
I will never let her escape again..."**

Driving along a dark road with
endless fields lining each side.
Headlights flickering as the full moon
floods the Earth with its luminescent glow.
A silhouette ahead and I am traveling alone.
Cautiously approaching, my breath stolen.
This ghostly stranger familiar,
bearing the face of my own.
Halting, I crack the window,
the cool dark air gifting me breath.
My eyes famished,
gorging on her every feature.
Her flawless features bear no
scars or imperfections,
eyes shine as opal in the sunlight,
and that smile---sending vibrations
of energy into the air that infiltrates the soul---
calming, resilient, full of hope and energy.

My voice imprisoned by the
constriction of my throat.
I have found her---
Me, before being crushed by
the heaviness of the world's burdens.
I was attacked so viciously by
hatred, bitterness, pain, and anguish
SHE FLED, and I,
I nursed those wounds.
But now, I have found her.
I have craved her light and
lusted for her beauty like a fiend.
She opens the door and I drink her in.
I will never let her escape again
for I would rather lose my life protecting her
than to be condemned to this
darkness once again.

"Untitled 12"
Lea Elani

"...But the wounds that hurt the most you won't see..."

In general pain or trauma is hard to deal with
Pain can result in both anxiety & depression
It can easily change a person's whole mood
This is something that people can conquer
Because at the end of the day as I see it
Everyone has a rather unique way to cope

My pain was the one who pulled the strings
I'd be at the full mercy of a master puppeteer
Thinking YOU get to dictate how life plays out
But you think that this is your own story to tell
This is a huge mistake on your behalf though
'Cause I am the one in control of my existence

You have consistently run my life like a dictator
But in my mind & soul the majority always wins
'Cause I get the role of the JUDGE in this house
So find me in contempt and toss me in a CELL
Yet I am the one who holds the key to escape
In here what I say is what goes no matter what

You have no say in the story that is MY life
Of course you will be a key component in it
Destroying key & iconic chapters in this BOOK
Yet if I wanted to I can erase you completely
If I did that it would be taking a part out of me
So you get an accompanying ROLE in this tale

This is no longer your complex game of chess
It is my life and I am tired of being your PAWN
I have walked along this dreary road once B4
I won't be treated like any untalented ROOKie
So you'd try to drag me back to the KNIGHT
And then I'll win the game with CHECKMATE
In my mind I will always fill the role of the KING

This is my life so I won't hand you the reins
'Cause I will always be who's in total control
You can gladly dwell inside of my mental hell
At the end of it I have to accept your presence
In a way you make up the one called Lone Wolf
Scars will serve as a reminder of the damage
But the wounds that hurt most you won't see...

"No More..."
Mike Cruz

"...anchors and shackles tied around my ankles."

today i caught my breath.
for the longest time i was suffocating,
but today i was able to gasp for air.
nobody saw me drowning in all of my sorrows
always wishing for a better tomorrow.
thinking about how i can keep afloat
instead i was keeping myself anchored
as i felt this anger
grow and grow
and that's what stopped me.

when i thought i was swimming to the shore
i was actually in the middle of nowhere.
lost.
still losing air.
not today, i will stop being afraid
of saying goodbye.
i will say goodbye
to those anchors and shackles
tied around my ankles.
i will breathe
because today i caught my first breath
and the same mistakes i refuse to make
i say goodbye to the life i knew
and say hello to a new muse.
me.

"Page 34"
Aly Maria

"Gratitude for all the things I thought would surely kill me..."

The life I was chosen to live is a gift.
A gift, that allows me the opportunity to transform
    pain and trauma into triumph!

Gratitude for all the things I thought would surely
>kill me, instead they made me typical when I
>thought I was unique.
Blessed with the awareness of knowing that I am not
>the only one. Others too have pain, trauma,
>despair, and desire, relief. I pray that through
>our collective journey of bleeding poetry we are
>all soon set free!

"Untitled 13"
LaDasha-Diamond

"I am healed, despite our encounters, as I SET aside the negative bane..."

GOODBYE delicious trauma, I was wrong
TO judge you too soon,
ALL the beauty you've brought to
MY life has not been in vain. This
PAIN has aided my perception
AND understanding---that
TORMENTS lead to epiphanies.

YOU are exactly what I needed, and you
WERE kind enough to enter my life. When I
NEEDED guidance, you appeared in my mind
FOR me to seek council.
MY greatest achievements brought about
TRANSFORMATION birthed from your fury.

BUT now it's time to let go,
NOW it's time to be free of your pain.
I am healed, despite our encounters, as I
SET aside the negative bane
YOU gave to me, so that one day I'd be
FREE.

"Free"
Sarrah Safi

"In this circle of karma, Why is it only striking back at us?"

In this Marvel Universe,
Why do we fall into the curse?
People full of Love and Prosperity,
Why do we have to deal hours feeling guilty?
In this circle of karma,
Why is it only striking back at us?
In need of happiness and peace,
Why is that we have to beg for mercy?
Families full of interactions, well beings,
Parenting and emotions,
When will we get those things into motions?

Grief, Anxiety, Depressed Essence are circumvented,
Why are we that are Emotionally Abused and Mentally Confused?
Igniting Fires and Burning Desires,
What are we supposed to do when we're not Liars?
Opera Houses and Theatres fully Empty,
Why is that our life's full of Tantrums and Drama?
Open Shy, desperate to Compensate,
Where is this nuisance coming from to make us
Upset?
Living what we have lived has been tough,
Getting to it that's not been enough,
Few more avenues are going to be awfully rough.

"In Need of Happiness and Peace"
Dhruvil Purani

"But if I hadn't executed my voice, I wouldnt know my resilience..."

If I hadn't executed my voice,
I would not have these wounds to mend,
to bandage them in shame and regret.
If I hadn't executed my voice,
my spirit wouldn't have been murdered by yours,
my strength never siphoned,
my legs never cut from under me.
If I hadn't executed my voice,
my child would not have this trauma to bear---
WE would not have these torments to heal.

But if I hadn't executed my voice,
I wouldn't know my resilience or
how to cherish this woman,
I would be condemned to the cycle of recycling me.
If I hadn't executed my voice,
I would never have found this pure unfiltered love
saturating with his healing touch.

"Untitled 14"
Lea Elani

"...resilience born in my heart, Resurrected in my spirit..."

I am writing this with blood on my lip,
And a final breath on my nib,
This poem will bleed my eulogy,
So pay close attention to the plot.

I'll start with a thank you to my heart,
Sharp waves were sent to cut her strings,
But she nurtured the love within her,
Whilst battling these storms,

She swam across testing hands of the clock,
And dived right into every ocean of 'I love you',
As her naive openness consumed her sense,

She tripped over demons,
Masquerading as their Queen,
Only just escaping fires,
Burnt but unseen.

And now I'll remember my spirit,
Oh! How she has shined throughout the dark,
Wrestling the moonlight to land among the stars,
Her damaged knuckles played their part,
Fighting for her rights,
And standing tall against her plights,

My bodacious spirit,
Romanticising pain and grief,
Letting them think they have her,
And then soaring right through their reefs,

Drinking from her own broken cup,
Never once announcing her needs,
Although scarred and wounded,
Determined to never lose her belief.

You may be thinking now,
What a resilient someone.
But even resilience,
Was once no one.

Resilience was conceived from trauma,
She was born in a battlefield,
She was barely walking before she had to fly,
She was raw and malnourished,
But fanatical and ambitious,

She was laughed at and bullied,
Stripped of her existence before she complained,
But she sustained...
She fought,
She persisted,
She rose.

She rose when everything and everyone was asleep,
And baptised herself with her name.

So, I may be gone soon.

But this resilience born in my heart,
Resurrected in my spirit,

She will stay.
Longer than her welcome.

You may visit her often,
And she will help you too,
To brazenly blossom.

"The poem that bleeds my Eulogy"
Nupur Nair

"We got this! We got this! We exclaim again and again..."

At 11pm around the bonfire,
we gather with paper lanterns,
wet tissues, and ready pens while
lugging our sacred yet caustic cares.
Then we attend to the heavy deed
of tossing our bad fathers, toxic exes,
terrible bosses, mean grannies,
malicious beauty standards, and
our debilitating accidents into
the roaring flames as we chant
our fuck yous and you can't wins
at them, essentially burning their
existence from our brains.
We hurl them into the inferno
one by one, corpse after corpse,
poem after poem, releasing
the hold on us they once had,
freeing ourselves from the viruses
they tried to infect us with, we do this
knowing that freedom is the cure...

There may be hurt that's residual,
but the pain is not nearly as sharp...
And after the arduous task of
bleeding, purging and crying,
we dance spryly and laugh lightly
around the passionate fire and
then commence to the craft of
writing hopes onto paper lanterns
releasing them into the limitless future
knowing our strength was fortified
by our bricks of resilience.
We got this! We got this!
We exclaim again and again
hearing whispers from angelic
moms and sisters singing our praise.
All rejoicing victoriously round
the bonfire assured that indeed we do,
we most certainly do, got this!

"Around the Bonfire They Meet"
Dara Kalima

AUTHORS

"Behind every poem are words. Behind those words are people."

Aly Maria is a 25-year-old Hispanic woman from The Bronx, NYC, one of the worst rumored cities to ever live in or visit. People are wrong though; she thanks her city for raising her and teaching her; without its roughness she wouldn't be so sensible. She was 15 when she turned to writing and it has been her escape ever since. She's had highs and lows, but it's never not worth turning into art. She is a proud mom to a beautiful 6-year-old girl who she wants to make proud of all that she does. Take a ride on her powerful journey through all her words as she hopes to reach and maybe inspire those who are too afraid, like she once was. Follow her on her page @alymariawrites.__ where she hopes to meet you all.

Anubis is a spoken word artist and cultural curator telling stories through poetry, hip hop, and theatre. He has been writing, performing, and advocating for the young people in his community his entire life. Anubis founded The Bomb Shelter: Harlem's Spoken Word Open Mic & Showcase which provided a stage for amateur and award-winning poets and performers as well as a place for young people to express thoughts and feelings that often reflect the woes of disenfranchisement and discontent with current social events.

Carla M. Cherry is an English teacher from New York. Her poems have appeared in *Anderbo, Eunoia Review, Dissident Voice, Random Sample Review, MemoryHouse Magazine, Bop Dead City, Terra Preta Review,* and *Anti-Heroin Chic.* She has published four books of poetry through Wasteland Press: *Gnat Feathers and Butterfly Wings (2008), Thirty Dollars and a Bowl of Soup (2017), Honeysuckle Me (2017),* and *These Pearls Are Real (2018).*

Cheree Alexander-Velez (pseudonym: Jereni-Sol) is a teaching artist, published poet, and a spoken word artist. She earned her Teaching Artist Certificate from Community Word's Teaching Artist Program, having interned at PS 279 in the Bronx and taught Poetry 101 to ESL adult students at the International Center in Manhattan. Cheree later founded and facilitated Poetry on Demand, a workshop that encouraged members to write, share and perform poetry. Her work can be found in several poetry anthologies including the *BX Writers Anthology* by Josue Caceres, *Broken Hearts-Healing Words* by Austie M. Baird, *Mind: A Poetry Anthology exploring mental health* by Poet Spotlight and *Poetry Pills: A Prescription for Goodness* by Paper Paints & Poetry, Janai V. Cheree has performed at several venues in New York City including the Nuyorican Poets Café, The Schomburg Center, Bronx Museum and Moca Lounge. Find her on Instagram @jerenisolpoetry.

Dara Kalima, also known as The Community Poet, is a loud and proud Bronx, New York resident who started writing at the age of 9, dedicated herself to the craft at 16, and locked into her poetic voice at 25. She has a BA in Drama Studies, MA in Educational Theater, and an MPA in Nonprofit Administration. Dara has performed on several stages across New York City including Bowery Poetry Cafe, the Nuyorican Poets Cafe, and Mike Geffner's Inspired Word. In 2018, she made her international debut, performing in Scotland. She founded and facilitates Black Authors Collaborative, a Facebook group dedicated to helping established and aspiring authors share resources and discuss publishing best practices. Dara has authored three books, *Black Man, Black Woman, Black Child (2015), Casualty of Love (2017)* and *Two X Chromosomes with an Extra Shot of Melanin (2019)*. To find out more about her, visit www.darakm.com.

Dhruvil Purani is an India based writer who enjoys writing poetry, blogs, and quotes. He is currently pursuing his Bachelor's Degree in Electrical Engineering, but that doesn't stop him from indulging in journal writing and sketching. Dhruvil began writing in 2017 and primarily writes about mental health and love. He has been published in several anthologies including *Clogged Impressions* published by Spectrum of Thoughts, *Stardust* published by Fanatixx Publications, and *Mirakee* published by Mirakee Publication. You can connect with Dhruvil on Instagram@shades_n_sayings and read his blogs at http://blogsbydap.wordpress.com.

Jessica Collazo is a Latina writer who resides in Brooklyn, New York. She has been writing poems since the age of 10, and honed her skills in creative writing courses at John Jay College of Criminal Justice. It was here that she also learned to infuse social justice influences into her writing. She loves coffee, reading, and listening to amazing playlists while writing. An introvert with an extrovert heart, Jessica writes poems about love, loss, identity, and the struggles of being a Latin woman. She can be found frequenting local open mic venues such as Open Mic Renegades. You can follow Jessica and her poetic musings on Instagram at @jessdoespoetry.

Keisha Molby-Baez also known by her poet name Coco is a writer, author, veteran, curator, mother of three and a Bronx Coordinator. Keisha is the author of two self-empowering poetry books *Tears laced with Fire* and *A little bit of Sugar.* Her poem "Seeds Planted" is published and featured in *MER VOX Quarterly.* Keisha's poems are anthologized in *Inside the Panic Room, United: Volume Red, BX Writers* and *The Revolution*, of which she is a Pushcart Prize nominee. Keisha is an incredible supporter and producer of her community. She has a lovely inner light and a raw-truth style that captivates her audience. She is the creator of Coco's Delight and dedicated to her life path of turning pain into purpose. She enjoys performing, challenging herself, and empowering others. Keisha is currently working on her third book and next project.

Kevin Ponder is a poet from Yonkers, NY. He works as a Field Tech Engineer for Dell Technologies, and is an avid gamer. He's been writing poetry since the age of 14, and mostly writes about love. His poems are often story driven pieces and comedic in nature. Within the last year, he has taken part in a variety of open mic and poetry slam venues, found an interest in erotica and inspirational poetry, as well as having been published in an anthology titled, *United Volume: Red.* He continues to push his poetry forward as he develops his own style while deriving inspiration from life experiences and learning from other poets that he's come to meet in his life.

LaDasha-Diamond is a community leader and artist who uses her own struggles and journey of self-determination to inspire individual and community resilience. Her work focuses on healing trauma so we can triumph and reclaim our ability to dream.

Latonica Readdy is an up and coming poet, author/novelist from the Bronx. She began writing poetry at the age of 13 years old, when she was exposed to Langston Hughes in school. Latonica's poetry is inspired by her lived experiences and world events. Her writing is also heavily influenced by Maya Angelou and Sonia Sanchez. She can be found performing her work at 10:02 Lounge's Bronx Poetry hosted by Shay G. To find out more about Latonica and her work you can tune in every Sunday to her podcast "Sunshine and Haiku" on anchor.fm or Spotify. You can also connect with her on Instagram at @herownstandards and @living_poetree.

Lea Elani is a Licensed Clinical Social Worker (LCSW) whose poetic writings focus on hardships and healing throughout life. With over two decades of writing about her own traumas and healing, she infuses both darkness and light into her work while also weaving in resonating emotions and life experiences. Lea's professional training in the mental health field has allowed her to further recognize how writing can facilitate one's own resilience and empowerment by processing personal trauma and pain. She can be contacted through her website, ww.leaelanipoetry.com, which displays her pieces, as well as the works of fellow writers.

Luna Brasa is a little fairy girl, making sense of the world through poetry. Located in the mythical mountainscapes of Denver, she uses writing to process the whirlwind of emotions brought on by day to day life and the general pains of human existence. She enjoys pushing the limits of her craft by participating in various writing challenges with a special shout-out going to @poetixuniversity and @tonii2eyes. Find her struggling through the purgatory of life on Instagram at @treeofembers or on Facebook at Luna Brasa Poetry.

Meka J. Woods was born in Bronx N.Y. but raised in South Jamaica, Queens. The Poet has become known for her simplistic word play and thought-provoking topics. Finding her poetic voice in 2017, J.Woods has made many strides toward success. She is a featured artist in many shows throughout NYC and has recently started her own show called The Hungry Poet TV Presents Fcukin Poets. Meka often states that the pen is the closest thing to her heart and the stage is her first true love.

Michael Isaiah Cruz is a Puerto Rican poet from Brooklyn, NY. He's been dabbling with writing and creating poetry for most of his life but truly dedicated himself to the craft about a decade ago. His writing has become an escape from the harshness of the real world. Michael may be quiet and unassuming in person but his way with words will quickly show you how dynamic he really is. You can connect with him on Instagram at @lonewolfpoetry7.

Nupur Nair, also known as 'The Dancing Ink' was born in India and raised in Dubai. While Nupur received her degree in Graphic Communication and Illustration from Loughborough University she has been in love with the written word for as long as she can remember. Nupur enjoys exploring a number of topics through her writing including mental health, nature, love, and the varying types of relationships people find themselves in. She utilizes different techniques and styles to enhance her writing like Japanese poetry, sonnets, acrostics, blackout poems, etc. Nupur feels most accomplished when she is able to connect and relate to others through her writing. She has been published in the *Tears of Swords* Anthology available on Amazon. You can connect with Nupur on Instagram at @Thedancingink.

Sarrah Safi's words are her calling/ language/ expression. She fell in love with writing at an early age and never stopped. Her ambition led to connections which then led to a writing career (politics, cannabis, health, medicine, business, etc.). But in April of 2020, the Poetix Bleed Challenge re-introduced her to the calling her soul was aching to express; poetry. She found a way to look at her past trauma and make sense of it. Her closing poem to the challenge helped her to overcome the hold her past pains had over her. Now she continues to write from her soul's perspective while living her best life in Colorado with her family.

Taneeka L. Wilder is a self-published author of *On the Precipice of Love Illuminated.* Taneeka uses her words to penetrate and nourish hearts for the purpose of healing, inspiration, and reflection. She has been interviewed on *Progressive Radio PRN. FM, LiveHip-Hop Daily,* and was also featured on the radio program *Midnight Meditations with CharLena,* and Mike Geffner's *Inspired Word NYC.* Taneeka has performed at various venues, and facilitated workshops on health, wellness, and healing. She is currently envisioning her next literary venture, with a second book in progress.

INDEX

Childhood

Classroom - Taneeka L. Wilder	2
Clear Vision: Always a Monster - Dara Kalima	4
Reach - Carla M. Cherry	6
Six - Meka J. Woods	8
3 Lies - Anubis	10
Fears Of Blur - Kevin P.	14
On High Alert - Mike Cruz	16
Page 32 - Aly Maria	18
Troubled Child - Latonica Readdy	22
Innocence Lost - Carla M. Cherry	24
She-Volution - Taneeka L. Wilder	26
Era of Teenage - Dhruvil Purani	28
Untitled 1 - Jessica Collazo	30
Page 26 - Aly Maria	32
Untitled 2 - Jessica Collazo	34

Loss

Untitled 3 - LaDasha-Diamond	38
Original Sin - Luna Brasa	40
Age 9: Loss of a Matriarch - Latonica Readdy	42
Just A Shy Kid - Luna Brasa	44
Mr. Reflection - Anubis	46
Untitled 4 - Jessica Collazo	48
A Letter to my Infector: You lose - Latonica Readdy	50
Dear Donna - Carla M. Cherry	54
Finding the cure - Nupur Nair	56
Untitled 5 - LaDasha-Diamond	58
Don't Cry For Me - Keisha Molby-Baez	60
Sun, Shadow & Space - Taneeka L. Wilder	64
I miss you - Cheree Alexander-Velez	66
Untitled 6 - Lea Elani	68
You Live In Me - Mike Cruz	70

Relationships

Counterfeit Love - Taneeka L. Wilder	76
If I Were A Leaf - Kevin P.	78
Hollow Girl - Jessica Collazo	80
Page 28 - Aly Maria	82
Love's Artifacts - Dara Kalima	84
Page 29 - Aly Maria	86
In my hands - Cheree Alexander-Velez	88
When Strangers Speak - Anubis	90
Ghost Girl - Luna Brasa	92
Premonition - Kevin P.	94
When 'Me' met 'She' - Nupur Nair	96
The Cure: Me - Dara Kalima	98
Me To Me - Meka J. Woods	100
Demolished Love - Latonica Readdy	102
A Short Story - Anubis	104

DNA - Sarrah Safi	*106*
A Bitter Memory - Kevin P.	*108*
Hard Truth - Cheree Alexander-Velez	*110*
Watering A Dead Rose - Keisha Molby-Baez	*112*
Untitled 7 - Lea Elani	*116*

Reflection

Untitled 8 - LaDasha-Diamond	*120*
An Ode To Self-Damnation - Luna Brasa	*122*
SEVEN - Nupur Nair	*124*
To: You - Sarrah Safi	*126*
When the sun sets - Cheree Alexander-Velez	*128*
Zombie - Sarrah Safi	*130*
Suddenly - Keisha Molby-Baez	*132*
The Heartbreak - Mike Cruz	*140*
Thank You, Ghosts - Sarrah Safi	*142*
Memorandum - Carla M. Cherry	*144*
The Cure - Keisha Molby-Baez	*146*
Untitled 9 - LaDasha-Diamond	*150*
Today - Jessica Collazo	*152*
Ladder - Anubis	*154*
Reality Is Bitch - Dhruvil Purani	*156*
Mrs. Hyde's Dark Valley - Latonica Readdy	*158*
Bad Perspectives - Mike Cruz	*160*
Bend - Carla M. Cherry	*162*

Healing

Untitled 10 - Lea Elani	*166*
Goodbye - Nupur Nair	*168*
Peace Out! - Cheree Alexander-Velez	*170*
Winning The Battle - Dhruvil Purani	*172*
Untitled 11 - LaDasha-Diamond	*174*
Flight 603 - Taneeka L. Wilder	*176*
Bleed Openly - Dhruvil Purani	*178*
Hand In Claw - Luna Brasa	*180*
Valediction - Keisha Molby-Baez	*184*
Released and Reformed - Dara Kalima	*188*
Good Riddance - Kevin P	*190*
Untitled 12 - Lea Elani	*192*
No More... - Mike Cruz	*194*
Page 34 - Aly Maria	*196*
Untitled 13 - LaDasha-Diamond	*198*
Free - Sarrah Safi	*200*
In Need of Happiness and Peace - Dhruvil Purani	*202*
Untitled 14 - Lea Elani	*204*
The poem that bleeds my Eulogy - Nupur Nair	*206*
Around the Bonfire They Meet - Dara Kalima	*208*

"Scars are stronger than the original skin."

-tonii

Bled

www.ingramcontent.com/pod-product-compliance
Lightning Source LLC
Chambersburg PA
CBHW071353290426
44108CB00014B/1532